Unveiled
A Christian Study Guide to Islam

www.isaac-publishing.us

1st English-language Europe edition

Published in the United States of America by Isaac Publishing

Isaac Publishing, 6729 Curran Street, McLean, VA 22101, USA

Printed in the United States of America

Copyright © 2011 Barnabas Fund

ISBN: 978-0-9825218-4-7

Contents

Introduction

This study guide has been written to help Christians to know what the religion of Islam teaches and to understand the world-view of Muslim people.

It is the first book in a planned series. Other titles in the series will focus on other subjects, such as how to share the love of Jesus with Muslims, how to care for converts from Islam, and comparing Islamic theology with Christian theology. Islam and Christianity are very different, as all the books will show. But Muslim people and Christian people are all human beings. Muslims and Christians value goodness and kindness and can live in peace together, as they have done for centuries in some places. Christians must always love Muslims with the love of Christ.

The aim of this study guide is for Christians to learn how different Islam is from Christianity and to be aware of how Islam has spread across the world, both in the past and now. The last chapter looks at how to share the Gospel with Muslims. Finally, there is a glossary explaining the meaning of some Islamic words. The chapters include Bible readings. These are there to give a Christian perspective on each chapter.

The guide can be used by an individual for personal study, or church leaders can use it to train a group, perhaps in 13 weekly sessions or at a training conference. An example of a time-table for a three-day training conference on Islam is given on page five. Each chapter of this study guide is complete on its own, so if there is not time to cover all the chapters, a group leader can choose the ones that are most useful for the group's needs.

At the end of each chapter there are questions, with space for answers to be written. If the study guide is being used to train a group, the leader should use the questions to create discussions and debates. These questions are only suggestions and a leader may wish to leave some out or add others.

If the material is to be used as a weekly study, leaders may think of structuring each weekly session as follows:

- Open the meeting with a prayer
- Recap last week's chapter
- Give a talk on this week's chapter
- Lead a group discussion using the questions as a guide
- Encourage prayer and worship

The leader will find it helpful to spend time in preparation before each session: to study the material well enough to give a talk on it, and to pray for the Lord's guidance and protection.

This guide briefly covers many areas and issues related to what Muslims believe and do. However, it is only a basic introduction. For those who would like to learn more about Islam, there are some suggestions for further reading below.

Further Reading

Patrick Sookhdeo, *A Pocket Guide to Islam*
Fearn, UK: Christian Focus Publications, 2010.
A simple guide to Islam that will help you understand why Muslims think and act as they do

Rosemary Sookhdeo, *Breaking Through the Barriers: Leading Muslims to Christ*
McLean, VA, USA: Isaac Publishing, 2010.
Useful teaching and practical help for sharing your faith with your Muslim neighbours

Rosemary Sookhdeo, *Why Christian Women Convert to Islam*
McLean, VA, USA: Isaac Publishing, 2007.
Explains the issues and problems faced by women who marry Muslims or become Muslims themselves

Gerhard Nehls, *Al-Kitab "The Book"*
Wellington, South Africa: Biblecor, (no date)
A Bible course to use with Muslims who are asking questions about Christianity or who have just become Christians

http://www.answering-islam.org
A very helpful Christian website that provides answers to many of the claims that Muslims make about Islam

Sample Time-Table

The following is an example of how a leader might plan a 3-day conference on Islam. The course could also be spread out over more days, with more time allocated to each topic and more time for discussions.

Time	Day 1	Day 2	Day 3
0900-0930	Devotions, Prayer and Worship	Devotions, Prayer and Worship	Devotions, Prayer and Worship
0930-1030	The Power and Love of God	The Five Pillars of Islam	Muslim Culture and World-view
1030-1130	TEA	TEA	TEA
1130-1230	The Life of Muhammad	Influences on Islam	Women in Islam
1230-1330	LUNCH	LUNCH	LUNCH
1330-1430	A Short History of Islam	The Quran and Muslim Traditions and Law	How Muslims view Non-Muslims
1430-1530	A History of Islam in Europe	Differences within Islam	How to Witness to Muslims
1530-1630	Discussion and Intercessory Prayer	Discussion and Intercessory Prayer	Discussion and Intercessory Prayer

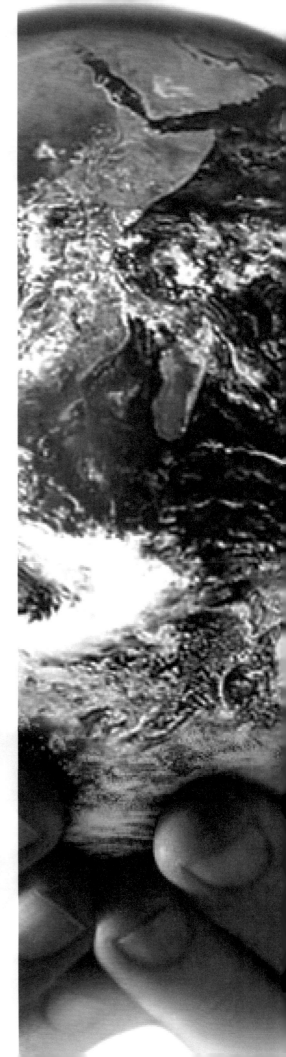

1

The Power & Love of God

Our God is Great

Read Psalm 33: 6-11.

God has created the heavens and the earth and everything that is in them. Scientists say that the known universe is many billions of light years across. A light year is how far light travels in a year, which is a very long way when you consider that light travels at 300 000 kilometres per second. The universe contains billions of galaxies and each galaxy contains billions of stars. It says in Genesis 1 that God just opened His mouth and spoke and this enormous universe was created.

God is powerful and is in total control of the universe. He controls the things we see and the things we can't. He is in control of powers, kingdoms, presidents, governments and world leaders. His power is so great that He could raise Jesus from the dead.

Our God is Very Personal

Read Ephesians 1: 3-5.

You may be wondering what the size of the universe has to do with Islam. Well, before we begin this series on Islam we need to make sure we know who our God is. The God Muslims believe in is a very powerful but very impersonal God. Muslims believe he is so distant that they can never have a personal relationship with him. Our God is not only huge and powerful and can do all things, but also He is a very personal God. He knows and cares about each one of us and the smallest details of our lives. He loves us and wants a personal relationship with us. He is a God of power and love. He sent His only Son to earth to die the most terrible death on the cross for you and for me so that our sins may be forgiven. He loves us that much. His Son did not die on the cross so that we could be His slaves. He died to set us free from sin and death so that we can be His sons and daughters. It is amazing that even before He created the heavens and the earth He had thought of us. We are the children of the God who just spoke and created the universe that is billions of light years across. As His children God's mighty power is at work within us through Jesus Christ. It says in Philippians 4: 13 that we can do all things through Christ who strengthens us.

The Difference between Islam and Muslims

Read 2 Corinthians 4: 1-6.

In this series on Islam we will learn many things about Islam. Some of what you learn may cause you to have some very strong emotions like frustration, helplessness, anger or even fear. Before we begin this study of Islam it is very important to understand the difference between Islam the religion and Muslims, the people who follow the religion. There are many different religions and beliefs across the world that claim that they are the only true religion. Islam Is one of these religions. However, Islam denies that Jesus Christ is God or that He died to save us from sin. It says in John 14: 6 that Jesus is the only way to the Father. This means that as Christians we believe there is only one true and real way of salvation and that is Jesus Christ. Any belief that says that Jesus is not God is a false belief.

In 2 Corinthians 4: 1-6 the Bible says that as Christians we must declare the truth and help all those who are trapped by false beliefs. It says in Corinthians that Satan has blinded many people from seeing the truth of Jesus Christ and His good news. It also says that those who Satan has blinded are perishing. If they do not hear and believe the Good News they will die eternally. We are told that we must preach Christ as Lord and Saviour to those who are perishing. So as Christians we must preach the Good News of Jesus Christ to Muslims who are trapped by Islam so that many may come to know Him as Lord and Saviour. Although we know that the religion of Islam is not according to Biblical truth, we must still love Muslims. Muslim people are like all other human beings on earth and are made in the image of God. They are trapped in the religion of Islam where they are very fearful and cannot find peace or be sure where they will go after they die. God loved the world so much that He sent His Son, Jesus Christ, to die on the cross so that all who believe in Him may be saved. So we know that God loves Muslims and wants them to be saved. As God's children we must show our Father's love to all people, including Muslims. In fact it says in 2 Corinthians 5:14 that Jesus died for everyone and it is His love that drives us to tell others about Him. All our interactions with Muslims should be done in love and compassion. There is no place for hatred, anger or fear in our relationships with Muslims.

Love not Fear
Read Luke 12: 4-12

Some Christians are very fearful of Islam. There are many things which cause this fear. Islam is spreading in Europe and the world at an alarming rate. The news is full of stories of issues relating to Islam, from the aftermath of September 11 to the wars in Iraq and Afghanistan. Islam is becoming more extreme and a growing number of Muslims believe in violence. There is more pressure on Christians and other non-Muslims who live in Muslim countries.

Remember that God is very very powerful and we are His children. As children of such a big God we have absolutely nothing to fear. He will look after us. Jesus tells us not to be afraid of what humans or evil powers can do to us. He loves us so much that He even knows how many hairs on our heads we have. If we love God we have nothing to fear from Him or from anything else.

He also tells us that we should love others just as He loves us. In fact our heavenly Father makes loving others a commandment. Jesus says in Mark 12: 31 that the two greatest commandments are to love God with all our heart, mind, soul and strength and to love our neighbour as ourselves. In this context neighbour means any and every person on earth. God wants His Kingdom on earth to be spread through love and forgiveness and not fear and hatred.

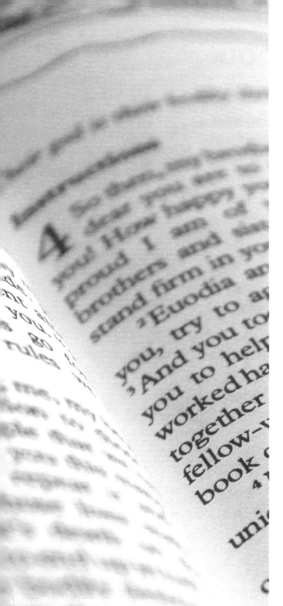

Spiritual Preparation

Read Ephesians 6: 10-18

Although we have nothing to fear, it is extremely important that we make sure that we are spiritually prepared before we study Islam. There are many lessons to learn from Ephesians 6: 10-18.

It starts off reminding us that the Lord is mighty and powerful and in Him we can be strong. God tells us that we do not fight against human beings and in our case Muslims. Remember we must love and pray for Muslims, not fight them. God tells us that we fight spiritually against the spiritual powers of the devil.

These spiritual powers are very real in Islam and we need to make sure we are protected in the Lord. We are told that we need to stand firm against these powers through truth and by living righteous lives. We must have faith in God and this faith will protect us from any attack by the devil. It says in 1 John 4: 4 that God who lives in us is greater than Satan who lives in the world. God will protect us because we are His children and He loves us. He has given us the weapon to fight against the evil spiritual powers and that is the Word of God. We need to make sure that we study the Word of God. The more we study it the more we will be able to stand against the devil and his schemes.

It is interesting that the Lord also tells us that our feet need to be fitted with readiness which comes from the gospel of peace. Although we are in a spiritual war the Lord tells us to always remember our purpose in this war; it is not destruction and violence, it is peace and love. Our role in this war is to spread the Good News about Jesus Christ and His love so that all those people who are lost may be saved.

Lastly we must pray continually. In this study we must pray in the Name of Jesus and ask for the protection of His shed blood over us. We must pray for each other for protection, courage, wisdom and a strong faith. We must pray for those Christians who are suffering under Islam. And we must pray for Muslims, those who are trapped by Islam so that they may come to faith in the Lord Jesus Christ and discover that God their heavenly Father is not only powerful but also loving.

Some questions to think about or discuss

- What picture do you have of God in your mind when you think of Him?

  ....

  ....

- How has your understanding of God and His greatness changed?

  ....

  ....

- How personal is our God?

  ....

  ....

- What do you think "understanding the difference between Islam and Muslims" means?

  ....

  ....

- Why must we not be fearful of Islam?

  ....

  ....

- What does Ephesians 6: 10-18 say we are fighting against?

  ....

  ....

- What are the many lessons that Ephesians 6:10-18 tells us about spiritual preparation?

  ....

  ....

- What should we pray for as part of our spiritual preparation?

  ....

  ....

2

The Life of **Muhammad**

What we Know about Muhammad

Before we begin to learn about Muhammad, it is important to remember that all we know about him comes from Muslim records which were written 150 years or more after his death. No one else had written about him or his life at that time. So there is no other evidence to suggest that the stories of Muhammad are true.

Muhammad's Early Life

Muhammad was born around 570 AD in the important trading town of Mecca. He was an Arab and most Arabs were pagans at that time. His family was well respected but very poor. His father died a few months before he was born and his mother died when he was only six. Muhammad's grandfather took care of him for two years before he too died. Muhammad was then put in the care of his uncle. Muhammad travelled with his uncle on trading trips and it is possible that he learnt about the religion of the Jews and Christians on these trips.

When Muhammad was a young man he worked for a very rich widow called Khadija. They were married when he was 25. She was 15 years older than him. They were married for 25 years before Khadija died. They had several children. However, only one child, his daughter Fatima, survived to adulthood. After Khadija died Muhammad married another twelve wives. One of them was only six years old. This made polygamy (many wives) acceptable in Islam. Although Muhammad believed he was allowed to have twelve wives, the Quran only allows other Muslims to have four wives at a time.

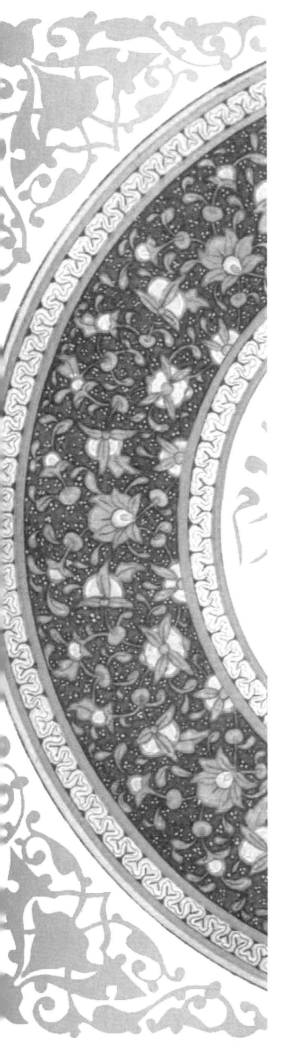

Muhammad Has Visions

After Muhammad married Khadija he did not have to work any more because she was so rich. He often spent time meditating in a cave near his house. He came back from one of his meditation times and told people that while he was in the cave he fell into a trance and saw some kind of heavenly being. Muhammad said that this being gave him a message directly from God to preach to humans. Muhammad told his wife about this experience and said that he was scared that he had seen a demon. However, she thought that he must have seen an angel. Muslims now claim that this "angel" was the angel Gabriel.

Over the years Muhammad said that he had many visits by this heavenly being. As Muhammad began telling people about his experiences a small group of people began to believe him and follow him. They called him a prophet and a messenger of God. Muhammad preached a mixture of Jewish, Christian and pagan beliefs, and one of his main themes was that there was only one God. However, the people of Mecca, where he lived, were pagans and did not like his message and became violent towards him and his followers. In 622 AD, he fled to a city, now called Medina, where he was warmly welcomed. Muhammad's move to Medina (the hijra) is very important to Muslims and the Muslim calendar starts from this year. It also gave rise to the hijra doctrine.

Muhammad Turns to War and Violence

The people of Medina accepted Muhammad's message. He became very powerful and influential as more and more people began to follow him. He united many of the warring tribes of Medina. It was because of this that the people of Medina made him their leader. Muhammad had changed from being a simple and relatively peaceful preacher to the powerful leader of a new Muslim city state. He was their ruler, law maker, judge, and military commander. Muhammad used his new military power to control and conquer all the areas around Medina.

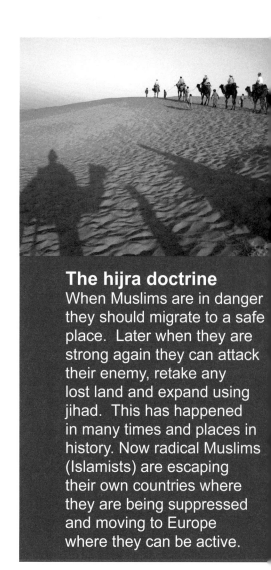

The hijra doctrine
When Muslims are in danger they should migrate to a safe place. Later when they are strong again they can attack their enemy, retake any lost land and expand using jihad. This has happened in many times and places in history. Now radical Muslims (Islamists) are escaping their own countries where they are being suppressed and moving to Europe where they can be active.

Muharram					December/January	
					Sat 1 19 Dec	**Sun** 2 20 Dec
on	**Tue**	**Wed**	**Thu**	**Fri**		
3 21 Dec	4 22 Dec	5 23 Dec	6 24 Dec	7 25 Dec	8 26 Dec	9 27 Dec
10 28 Dec	11 29 Dec	12 30 Dec	13 31 Dec	14 1 Jan	15 2 Jan	16 3 Jan
17 4 Jan	18 5 Jan	19 6 Jan	20 7 Jan	21 8 Jan	22 9 Jan	23 10 Jan
24 11 Jan	25 12 Jan	26 13 Jan	27 14 Jan	28 15 Jan	29 16 Jan	30 17 Jan

Muslims have a different calendar from ours. The Christian calendar is based on the sun and begins from the birth of Christ. The Islamic calendar is based on the moon and begins in the year Muhammad moved to Medina, which is 622 AD in our calendar. The Islamic years are only 354 days long instead of 365 or 366

Muhammad and Christians and Jews

Muhammad believed that he was sent by God as the final prophet of the Jews and Christians. He had even chosen Jerusalem as the direction of prayer for Muslims. Muhammad at first tried to convert Christians and Jews peacefully to Islam. However, because his message was so different from their beliefs and was also so full of pagan and many other beliefs and customs, they could not accept it. This made him extremely angry. He changed the direction of prayer from Jerusalem to Mecca. It was at this time that the messages in Muhammad's "visions" stopped being peaceful towards Jews and Christians and became harsh and violent. He massacred hundreds of Jewish men and enslaved their families.

After the Jews and Christians had rejected him, Muhammad led his army to Mecca. He conquered the town and declared that this was the centre of Islam.

Muhammad's Death and Legacy

Muhammad died in 632 aged about 62. He was succeeded by one of his closest followers, called Abu Bakr. Abu Bakr followed Muhammad's example of violence and used holy war or jihad to force people to accept Islam as their religion or to submit as second-class citizens. Islam spread rapidly.

Muslims believe that Muhammad was the perfect man. Everything that he did and taught was perfect and his life must be used as an example of how to live. This is why many Muslims still believe that Islam must be spread violently and through jihad.

Read 1 Peter 1: 16-22.
As Christians we know that Christ was the only man who ever lived who did not sin. He died for our sins. We are asked to follow Him and His example. To be like Christ we must love one another deeply and with all our hearts and spread His message through love not violence.

Some questions to think about or discuss

- When did Muslims first start writing about Muhammad and his life?

  ....
  ....

- Why must we question whether the stories written about Muhammad are true?

  ....
  ....

- What did you find interesting about Muhammad's early life?

  ....
  ....

- Why is polygamy (many wives) acceptable in Islam?

  ....
  ....

- What did Muhammad say happened in the cave where he was meditating?

  ....
  ....

- Did the people of his home-town Mecca accept his message? What happened?

  ....
  ....

- Was Muhammad accepted in Medina? What happened there?

  ....
  ....

- What changes happened to Muhammad in Medina?

  ....
  ....

- How did Muhammad view Jews and Christians at the beginning and how did this change?

  ....

  ....

- Do we see a similar attitude to Jews and Christians by Muslims today?

  ....

  ....

- Why do you think Muslims carry out jihad?

  ....

  ....

- What do you think about Muslims using Muhammad as the "perfect" example to follow?

  ....

  ....

- Read 1 Peter 1: 16-22. As Christians who is our example?

  ....

  ....

- How does the Christian example of Christ differ from the Muslim example of Muhammad?

  ....

  ....

3

A Short History of Islam

After Muhammad's Death

Muhammad died in 632. He was succeeded as caliph (leader of the Muslim community) by Abu Bakr, who was one of Muhammad's closest followers. Abu Bakr wanted Islam to spread wider than just Arabia and so he began fighting against many of the surrounding countries. Abu Bakr died in 634 and was succeeded by Umar. Umar was assassinated in 644. He was succeeded by Uthman who was also assassinated in 656. Uthman was replaced by Ali. This caused a huge split in the Islamic community because some Muslims did not want Ali to be the leader. A civil war began that lasted five years until Ali too was assassinated. The minority who accepted Ali and his descendants as leaders became known as Shia Muslims. The main body of Muslims became known as Sunni Muslims.

Despite all the disagreement, assassinations, civil war and violence Muslims look back at this time as the "Golden Age" of Islam. They also call this the age of the four "Rightly Guided Caliphs" (the four being: Abu Bakr, Umar, Uthman and Ali).

Islam Expands

One of the reasons that Muslims consider this time in their history to be the Golden Age is because it was a time when Islam spread very quickly. The four caliphs used their Muslim armies to conquer vast areas. During their leadership Islam spread to Palestine, Syria, Iraq, Persia, Egypt and North Africa. Most of these areas had very strong Christian communities which were weakened by the violent Muslim invasions.

This spread of Islam was seen as a holy war or jihad. Muslims believed that God had told them to make all people submit to Islam. Once an area was conquered large numbers of Muslims from Arabia would migrate into it. This helped to make sure that there was complete domination by Islam in an area. By 750 AD the Muslim empire stretched from Spain and Morocco in the west, to India and China in the east. It is very clear that Islamic rule was spread by the sword. Many of those who did not submit to Islam were killed. In many countries those who were not Muslims were enslaved or were treated as second class citizens. In the following centuries, a series of Muslim empires rose and fell in different parts of the world.

Beginning in the 12th century Islam spread throughout south-east Asia including today's Malaysia, Indonesia and Thailand. Muslims used trade as a way of winning converts to Islam. Many trade and shipping routes became Muslim controlled. Muslims were also very keen slave traders. Many Muslims moved to Africa to capture slaves and to win converts. This is why many of the African coastal regions and old slave routes are still Muslim today.

From the 14th to the 16th centuries, the Muslim Ottoman Empire expanded from its base (modern Turkey) into Europe. The Ottoman Empire lasted more than four centuries. Many Christian areas were conquered and invaded by the Ottoman Empire as it spread into parts of Europe, the Middle East and North Africa. At its strongest the Empire stretched from Austria in Europe through Turkey, the eastern Mediterranean, the Arabian peninsula to Algeria. It was finally defeated in the First World War.

Islamic expansion under Muhammad, 622–632

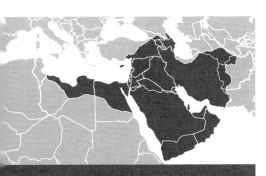

Islamic expansion, 632   661

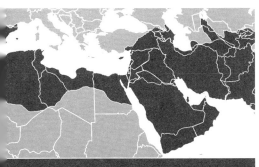

Islamic expansion, 661–750

The Crusades

During the early history of Islam many Christians began to worry about the speed at which Islam was spreading into Christian areas. The Holy Land, and other Christian areas such as Syria, Egypt, North Africa and Spain, were now under Muslim control. The Christian Byzantine Empire was being attacked, invaded and settled by Turkish Muslim tribes. France and Portugal were already under pressure. It seemed that, unless something could be done, all of Europe would fall to Islam. Also the Christians who were living in the conquered areas were pleading to their fellow Christians in Europe to help them against their Muslim invaders and attackers.

In 1096 Christians in Europe finally decided to do something and they sent an army to the Middle East to stop the persecution of Christians. This was the First Crusade. A total of nine crusades took place over a period of 200 years. The Christians were successful at first but later the Muslims gradually took back control of the area, including Jerusalem.

The Crusades were a very violent time for both Christians and Muslims. Many terrible things were done by both sides during these wars.

Muslims and many Westerners nowadays are very quick to blame Christians and Europe for the Crusades. Muslims often say that they were living in peace when armies from Europe attacked them. Muslims frequently demand that Christians and Europe apologise for the Crusades. Christians and Westerners are sometimes very quick to apologise. Muslim countries offer no apologies in return although it was the Muslims who had first invaded Christian areas. The Crusades were really a much delayed counter-attack, responding to centuries of Muslim jihad that had involved invading Christian lands and killing and persecuting Christians.

Islam Today

Islam is now the world's second largest religion, after Christianity. There are more than 1.4 billion Muslims in the world. Although one in four people in the world are Muslim, less than 15% of these are Arabs. The largest populations of Muslims are found in South Asia and in Africa. Almost 50 countries in the world have populations that are majority Muslim. There are 57 countries who are members of the Organisation of the Islamic Conference (OIC), though some of these member countries do not have Muslim majorities. In Europe, Turkey and Albania are members of the OIC, while Russia and Bosnia-Herzegovina have observer status. The OIC is the second largest intergovernmental organisation in the world after the United Nations. It is extremely powerful and influential, and offers political and economic benefits to its members.

Nowadays Islam mainly expands through trade and business, politics, legal changes, mass migration, marriage, conversion, and in some cases violence and terrorism. They often use economic aid to win converts in poor countries.

Christians need to be aware of all the ways that Islam is able to gain strength in their areas. As Christians we must pray for God's wisdom, strength and protection to resist the influences of Islam in their areas. We must become more involved in areas of business, education, politics and media so that Christians issues are represented. One of the causes of Islam spreading in the world today is Christians not being involved in society as much as they should be. However, we must always remember to act in Christ's peace and love towards Muslims in all that we do.

The Siege of Constantinople. Constantinople was a very important Christian city that was taken by the Muslim Ottomans in 1453. See page 23

19

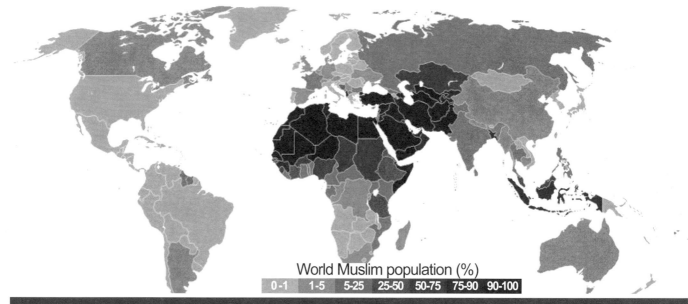

World Muslim population (%)

| 0-1 | 1-5 | 5-25 | 25-50 | 50-75 | 75-90 | 90-100 |

Map showing Muslim populations today

Read Matthew 22: 34-40 and Matthew 28: 18-20.
Jesus teaches us that the greatest commandment is to love the Lord our God with all our heart, mind and soul. He also tells us to love our neighbour. Jesus then tells us that He has given us the authority to go and spread the good news to all the nations on earth. We are to teach them all that Jesus commanded us to do, which was to love. Jesus told us to spread Christianity in love. Luke 4:18 says that Jesus came to set the captives free.

Some questions to think about or discuss

- Who were the four "Rightly Guided Caliphs" and how did they die?
  ....
  ....

- What do Muslims call the time that the caliphs ruled?
  ....
  ....

- Why do you think that they call this time by this name?
  ....
  ....

- What do Muslims believe God told them to do to non-Muslims?
  ....
  ....

- How were Christians and other people treated after they had been conquered by the Muslims?
  ....
  ....

- What did a number of Arabs usually do once an area was conquered?

....

....

- How was Islam spread to parts of Africa?

....

....

- Why did the Crusades happen?

....

....

- Why do you think that Muslims try to blame the Crusades on Christians?

....

....

- What do we have to remember about the Crusades?

....

....

- How big was the Ottoman Empire?

....

....

- When were the Ottomans finally defeated?

....

....

- How many Muslim countries are there in the world today? How many in Europe?

....

....

- How is Islam spreading today?

....

....

- What is your experience of Islam spreading in Europe?

....

....

- Read Matthew 22: 34-40 and Matthew 28: 18-20. As Christians how does the Lord Jesus tell us to spread His Kingdom?

....

....

- How does this differ from how Islam is spread?

....

....

4

A History of Islam in Europe

After Muhammad's death in 632, Muslim armies moved out of the Arabian Peninsula. They fought a jihad to try to bring Islam to many lands including Europe. At this time much of Europe had a strongly Christian heritage where almost everyone called themselves Christian, unless they were Jewish. Muslim writers often say that the Islamic conquests brought freedom and tolerance and that no one was forced to convert to Islam. This was sometimes true, but more often the conquered people suffered oppression and violence. Sometimes the Muslim conquerors destroyed cities and churches, took land and other property, and imposed heavy taxes. Sometimes they killed many ordinary people or turned them into slaves or forced them to become Muslims. Many Muslims also settled in the newly conquered lands.

Early Expansion

The Christian Byzantine Empire ruled over large parts of south-eastern Europe, and its capital Constantinople was at the meeting point of Europe and Asia. Its lands included Anatolia, Syria, Palestine, Egypt, parts of North Africa and some Mediterranean islands. Most of these exept Anatolia were soon conquered by the Muslim armies. Some of the conquered lands then became launch pads for attacks on Europe.

1. Mediterranean Islands and Italy
In the middle of the 7th century, the Muslims began to attack islands like Cyprus, Sicily, Rhodes and Crete, and later the Balearic Islands, Corsica and Sardinia. Some of these islands were fought over again and again, ruled sometimes by Muslims and sometimes by Christians.

The Muslims were also attacking Italy, and temporarily conquered Rome in 846. By the 10th century they were raiding in the lower slopes of the Alps in northern Italy.

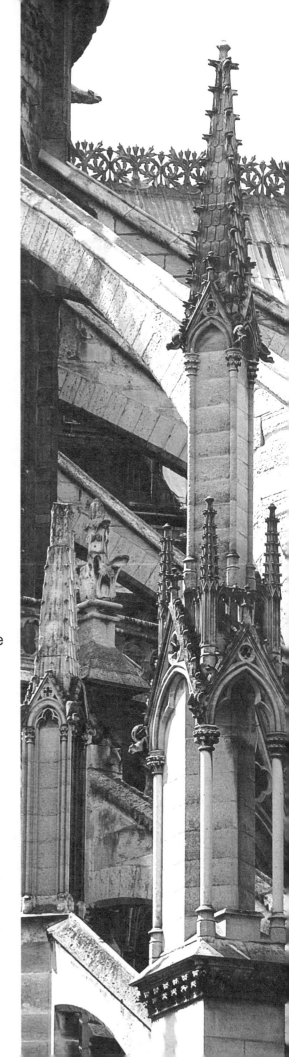

Arab and Berber conquests

Seljuk and Ottoman conquests

Christians, Muslims and Jews in Europe

Sadly, Europe has a long history of being anti-Jewish, and Jews were despised and suppressed by the Christian majority. But Europe's relationship with Islam was different, because for many centuries Christians and Muslims mainly interacted through violence and conflict – first the Muslim invasions of Europe and then the European colonisation of Muslim lands. It was only when Muslims began to migrate to Europe in large numbers in the 20th century that new social dynamics developed, with Muslims trying to find their place in a largely secular Europe.

2. Spain, Portugal and France

In the 8th century, the Muslims began to target what is now Spain, Portugal and southern France. Spain was invaded by Muslim armies from North Africa in 710. In an eight-year campaign most of Spain and Portugal, except for small areas in the north, was conquered by the Muslims. The conquest was accompanied by much looting and the killing of prominent Christians, soldiers, civilians and even children. The Muslims then crossed into France, but in 732 they were defeated there by Charles Martel in the battle of Tours-Poitiers. But Muslim armies continued to attack France.

There were short periods of time when Christians and Jews were treated well in Muslim Spain and coexisted peacefully with their Muslim rulers. But most of the time the Christians and Jews were discriminated against and sometimes persecuted.

3. The Ottoman Empire (1301-1922) in the Balkans and South-East Europe

By the 12th century, Turkish armies and migrating tribes had taken most of Anatolia from the Christian Byzantines. The Ottoman Empire developed, which saw itself as an Islamic state that must keep fighting unbelievers, especially the Christians in Europe. In 1352 the Ottomans gained their first foothold in Europe, occupying a fortress on the European shore of the Dardanelles. Ottoman armies continued to invade Europe and by the end of the 14th century they were moving into the Balkans and occupying northern Greece, Macedonia and Bulgaria. They defeated the Serbs at the Battle of Kosovo (1389).

After many attempts, the Ottomans finally captured Constantinople from the Byzantines in 1453. This was a turning point in history. Constantinople, renamed Istanbul, became the capital city of the Ottoman Empire. The Ottomans then conquered all of Greece.

For several centuries Ottoman armies, based in the Balkans, threatened central Europe. The best Ottoman troops, the Janissaries, were Christian boys from the Balkans who had been forcefully taken from their families, converted to Islam, and trained as soldiers. In the 16th century the Ottomans conquered much of Hungary. Twice they reached the gates of Vienna (1529 and 1683). After the defeat and retreat of the Ottomans following the second siege of Vienna, Ottoman power began to decline, though the Empire remained until after the First World War when modern Turkey was formed (1922-24).

The Ottoman soldiers received rewards for raiding Christian territory and providing a constant flow of captives for the Ottoman army and slave markets. Many of the captives died during forced marches.

In areas under Ottoman rule some indigenous Christians converted to Islam for a variety of reasons. The majority of Albanians and Bosnians became Muslims, either for protection or for economic or social advantages, or because they were forced to convert. Christians suffered discrimination under Ottoman rule.

4. The Tatars in Eastern Europe

A further threat to Europe came in the 13th century from the east when the Mongols under Genghis Khan conquered much of Russia and eastern Europe (Ukraine, southern Poland, Hungary and Bulgaria). They established a state known as the Khanate of the Golden Horde.

Berke Khan, grandson of Genghis Khan and leader of the Golden Horde, converted to Islam. The Mongols then became an Islamic power, and brought a new phase of Islamic expansion to Russia and eastern Europe. They were known as Tatars. In 1382 the Golden Horde sacked and burned Moscow, carrying off thousands of its inhabitants as slaves.

In the late 15th century the Khanate of the Golden Horde broke up into several smaller khanates based in Kazan, Astrakhan, Siberia and Crimea, but Tatar raids on Christian territory continued for several centuries.

The Russian tsar Ivan the Terrible conquered Kazan in 1552 and Astrakhan in 1556. The Siberian Khanate submitted in 1598. But the Crimean Khanate survived as an ally of the Ottoman Empire, and continued to raid into Russia and eastern Europe.

In 1671 Tatars and Ottomans joined forces and invaded Poland. The great Polish leader Jan Sobieski beat the Tatar-Ottoman troops, but in the end he was forced to sign a truce with them, giving up territory and promising to pay tribute. By 1680 his kingdom of Poland-Lithuania had been reduced to half its size. In 1783, Catherine the Great annexed the Crimean Khanate to the Russian Empire. She gave Tatar nobles equal rights with Russian nobles and

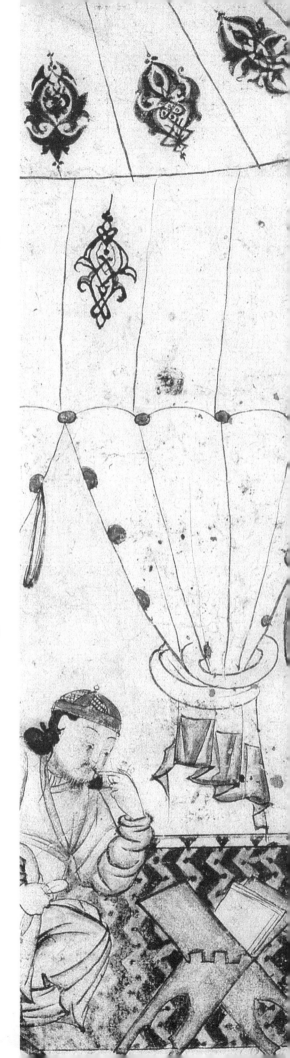

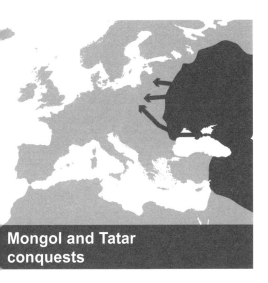

Mongol and Tatar conquests

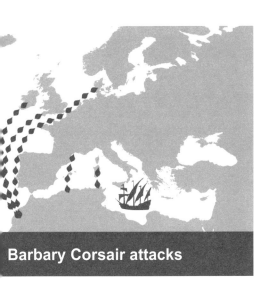

Barbary Corsair attacks

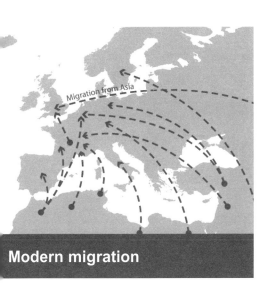

Migration from Asia

Modern migration

encouraged Tatar merchants to trade between Russia and Central Asia. The Tatars of the Golden Horde survive today in the Russian republics of Tatarstan and Bashkortostan as well as in the Crimea (in Ukraine) and the Caucasus. Small Tatar communities also remain in Poland and Lithuania.

5. Naval Jihad

After the Crusades, the Ottomans renewed their attacks in the Mediterranean. They raided southern Italy and re-conquered islands like Rhodes and Cyprus. In 1565 they attacked Malta with huge forces, but did not succeed in taking it. In 1571 the combined navies of Spain, Venice and the Pope defeated the Ottoman navy at the Battle of Lepanto.

Another important part of the Muslim naval jihad was carried out by Muslim pirates based in North Africa. Later known as "Barbary Corsairs" and allied to the Ottomans, they targeted European states in the Mediterranean and the Atlantic, going as far north as England, Ireland and Iceland. They attacked not only ships but also coastal towns. They captured large numbers of Europeans, who were sold as slaves in North Africa.

The corsairs justified their activities by describing them as a jihad against the non-Muslims. Their attacks lasted for many centuries, until Western naval forces stopped them in the 19th century.

European Responses

1. The Reconquista (8th-15th centuries) The small Christian kingdoms gradually re-conquered the Iberian Peninsula (Spain and Portugal) from the Muslims. The process was completed in 1492 with the fall of Granada to Ferdinand of Aragon and Isabella of Castile.

2. The Crusades (11th-13th centuries) The Crusades were a response to over 400 years of Islamic attacks on Christians. See page 18.

3. The European Colonial Expansion (16th-20th centuries) By the end of the First World War most Muslim countries were under European colonial control, whether Spanish, Portuguese, Dutch, French, British or Russian. Muslims deeply resented the colonial expansion and the control of their land by non-

Muslims. But by the 1960s all Muslim countries had regained their independence.

Islam in Europe Today

Since the 1960s large numbers of Muslims have been migrating to western Europe, mostly to try to improve their own economic status. Muslim populations in Europe are growing much faster than non-Muslim ones. As well as immigration, there are non-Muslims converting to Islam, but the main reason is that Muslim families have more children. Muslims often choose to live close together, so there are parts of some European cities which are almost totally Muslim.

A small proportion of Muslims in Europe are radicals (see pages 40-41), also called Islamists. They want to Islamise Europe, change its culture, and gain political power for Islam. They are often led by well-educated Muslims born in the West. They try to get sharia law introduced, encourage Islamic finance, set up Islamic schools, and try to prevent anyone from criticising Islam or Muhammad even as a joke. They are very active in universities, trying to radicalise students and also trying to control the academic teaching. There have been some threats of violence and occasionally actual violence, such as rioting and assassinations.

Slavery

Millions of Europeans were taken as slaves by Muslims. Thousands were taken from Moscow by Tatars in the 14th century. Hundreds of thousands were taken by the Ottomans in the middle of the 15th century, especially from Constantinople. From the 15th century to the early 17th century an estimated 500,000 to 1 million Christian boys from the Balkans were taken to be trained as Janissaries for the Ottoman army. At least a million Europeans were taken by the Barbary Corsairs between the 16th and 18th centuries; many were worked to death, but some were bought back with money specially collected by European churches.

Read Galatians 6: 9-10.
God teaches us to never grow tired of doing good. We are to make sure that we look after the Body of Christ. We must encourage each other in word and deed. It is also important that we do good to everyone, believers and unbelievers. It says in 1 Peter 2: 9-12 that Christians are a "holy nation" belonging to God. He tells us that we must live good lives full of Christ's love and kindness so that those unbelievers we come into contact with may become saved too. God intends the Good News to be spread and His "holy nation" to grow through love, kindness and forgiveness.

Some questions to think about or discuss

- When did Islam first come to Europe?

....

....

- How many European countries can you name that have been attacked or conquered by Muslim armies in the past?

   ....

   ....

- How were the European Christians and Jews normally treated by their Muslim rulers?

   ....

   ....

- Was it the same in Spain? If it was different was that all the time, most of the time, or just a small part of the time?

   ....

   ....

- How were Jews and Muslims treated by European Christians when the Christians were in power over them?

   ....

   ....

- There were two great Muslim powers that ruled parts of Europe for many centuries. What were they called, where did they rule, and where can you find their descendants today?

   ....

   ....

- Many Europeans were captured by Muslims and made into slaves. Which were the main Muslim groups who enslaved Europeans?

   ....

   ....

- How did Europe re-gain territory from Muslims or stop them advancing further?

   ....

   ....

- Do you think that Europeans were right to respond like that? If not, can you think of any examples of how the advance of Islam has been successfully stopped by other methods?

   ....

   ....

- Why are Muslim populations in Europe today growing so much faster than the indigenous European populations?

   ....

   ....

- Read Galatians 6: 9-10 and 1 Peter 2: 9-12. Islam was spread in Europe by violence in the past, and by other means today. How does God say Christianity should be spread?

   ....

   ....

The
Five
Pillars
of Islam

A Religion of Works

Muslims believe that when they die all their good deeds will be put on a scale and weighed against all their bad deeds. If their bad deeds weigh more then they will go to hell and suffer terrible torments for a time before they go to paradise (heaven). If their good deeds weigh more, and if God wills it, then they could go straight to paradise. But they cannot be certain, because it all depends on God's choice. Some think that people who die in jihad will go straight to paradise but, all in all, Muslims can never be sure that they will avoid hell. This is why many Muslims live in fear.

In order to make their good deeds weigh more Muslims are required to perform five duties. Muslims believe that if they do not perform these duties the chance of them going to hell is much higher. These duties are called the Five Pillars of Islam. They must also obey Islamic law (sharia).

1. Declaring the Faith

The declaration of faith is called shahada. It simply means to testify. Muslims must regularly testify or say what they believe. This is what they have to say, in Arabic: **I testify that there is no god but God and that Muhammad is the apostle of God.** Muslims believe that in order for someone to become a Muslim they just have to repeat the declaration of faith three times in front of two witnesses.

2. Prayer

In Islam, God is distant and impersonal. When Muslims pray it is a ritual and they are not sure if God will even listen to their prayers.

Muslims have to perform all kinds of rituals before and during their prayers. Muslims believe that they have to be physically clean before they can pray. They have to wash certain parts of their body, like their hands, head, face, teeth, mouth, beard, feet and toes. They must even rinse their nostrils out because they believe that when they sleep the devil stays in their nose. If they do not do these ablutions properly they believe that their prayers will not be counted as a good deed.

When Muslims pray they have to face towards Mecca. Their heads must also touch the ground. They have certain prayers that they must recite. The prayers are said in Arabic. Many Muslims all over the world, who cannot speak Arabic, do not even know the meaning of what they are saying when they pray.

Muslims have to pray five times a day. These are: at dawn; soon after midday; mid-afternoon; soon after sunset; and after nightfall. Muslims consider Friday to be their holy day. Men should go to the mosque for midday prayers on Friday, where they will often hear the imam (or mosque leader) preach before they perform their prayers.

In areas where there is a mosque you often hear a call to prayer in Arabic. It is common for Muslims to use loudspeakers to broadcast the call to prayer as far as possible. Muslims believe that wherever the sound of the call to prayer is heard that area is claimed for Islam.

The call to prayer is usually:
"God is great. I testify that there is no god but God and that Muhammad is the apostle of God. Come to prayer; come to success."
For early morning prayer these words are added:
"Prayer is better than sleep."

A Muslim prayer position

Christian prayer is very different from Muslim prayer. As Christians when we pray we have direct contact with God. We consider prayer to be a personal conversation with God. We do not have to wash before we pray because God accepts us with love no matter how dirty we are.

3. Fasting

Fasting is a very important part of Islam. It is done during Ramadan, which is the ninth month of the Islamic calendar. Ramadan starts at the first sighting of the new moon and ends at the first sighting of the new moon of the next month.

Muslims fast during Ramadan to remember when Muhammad was supposed to have had his first vision of the angel Gabriel.

For Muslims fasting means no eating, drinking, smoking or sex from sunrise to sunset during the whole month of Ramadan. However, as soon as the sun goes down each day, Muslims change from fasting to feasting. It is common for Muslims to feast until two in the morning. Then they get up early to eat again before sunrise. Muslims often eat more during the month of Ramadan than they would during normal months.

Willingly breaking the Ramadan fast during the day is considered extremely bad. Apart from the fear of going to hell, severe punishment is often imposed on those who break their fast. Even in some Muslim countries today if someone is caught breaking their fast they have to pay heavy fines or they may be beaten or even imprisoned.

Ramadan falls at a different time on our calendar every year. This is because of the difference between the Muslim calendar and the Christian calendar.

4. Giving

Muslims believe that if they give money to support Islam and help poor Muslims, then they have a better chance of going to paradise. Sunni Muslims must give 2.5% of all they earn and can give more in voluntary donations.

5. Pilgrimage to Mecca

All Muslims must travel to Mecca at least once in their life time if they can afford it. This pilgrimage is called the Hajj and happens during the twelfth month of the Muslim calendar. Mecca is considered the Muslim Holy City. In Mecca there is a large cubic structure called the Kaaba, which the pilgrims have to walk around seven times. Sometimes, while walking around the Kaaba, Muslims touch and kiss the Black Stone that is built into the corner of the Kaaba. The Black Stone is probably a meteorite. It was worshipped by pagans before Islam began but is now considered one of Islam's most holy objects.

A Muslim who has visited Mecca is called a hajji and is highly respected by other Muslims.

The Kaaba

Jihad (holy war), a Sixth Pillar?

The Islamic source texts (Quran and hadith) include many passages that glorify fighting for God and Islam in a holy war (jihad). Sharia says jihad is one of the most basic religious duties. A growing number of Muslims believe that fighting a jihad is such an important duty that it is the sixth pillar of Islam. This is why some Muslims are willing to become terrorists.

Muslims divide the world into two:
1. Places where Muslims rule. These places are called the House of Islam (Dar al-Islam).
2. Places where Muslims do not rule. These places are called the House of War (Dar al-Harb).

Muslims are supposed to fight a jihad to change the House of War into the House of Islam.

According to traditional Islam, jihad is God's way to expand Islam's rule. The caliph (Muslim leader) was required to lead an army in jihad against non-Muslims at least once a year.

Some Muslims reject this view and explain jihad as the internal moral and spiritual fight against sin. Most Muslims today agree that jihad is a religious duty to defend Islam, Muslims and Muslim territory from any form of aggression.

Six Articles of Faith
Muslims must believe in

- **God, who is one. This belief is called tawhid.**

- **Angels**

- **Holy books, but only Quran valid today**

- **Prophets, but only Muhammad to be followed today**

- **The Day of Judgement**

- **God's will decides everything**

Read Ephesians 2: 1-10.
The Bible teaches us we are all sinners. However, God loved us so much that He sent His Son, Jesus, to die for the forgiveness of our sins. Because of the grace of God and the sacrifice of Jesus on the cross we can be sure that we are forgiven and saved if we accept Jesus as our Lord and Saviour. We are saved not by good works but by grace.

Some questions to think about or discuss

- What do Muslims believe happens to them when they die?
  ....

  ....

  ....

- Can you name the five pillars of Islam?
  ....

  ....

  ....

- What do you think the difference is between Muslim prayer and Christian prayer?
  ....

  ....

  ....

Islam is a religion of works

- What do Muslims have to do before they pray?
  ....

  ....

- How often do Muslims have to pray?
  ....

  ....

- During which month do Muslims fast?
  ....

  ....

- When they are fasting what are Muslims not allowed to do from sunrise to sunset?
  ....

  ....

- What happens after sunset?

....

....

- What could happen if someone breaks a fast?

....

....

- How much should a Muslim give to the poor?

....

....

- Where must a Muslim go on pilgrimage at least once in their lives?

....

....

- What do they have to do once they are there?

....

....

- What is the Black Stone?

....

....

- What is sometimes called the sixth pillar of Islam?

....

....

- What are the six things Muslims must believe?

....

....

- Read Ephesians 2: 1-10. What do you think grace means?

....

....

- How is a Christian saved?

....

....

- How does this differ from Islam?

....

....

6

Influences on Islam

In this chapter we learn that Islam was influenced by many traditions, rituals and beliefs from other religions that already existed. The main religions in Arabia during Muhammad's time were paganism, Judaism and Christianity. Muhammad himself grew up as a pagan, but he met Jews and Christians when he went on trading trips. Paganism is the traditional religion that was practised by the many Arab tribes at that time. They usually worshipped the sun, stars, moon, ancestors, spirits and false gods. There are also some things in Islam that are very similar to paganism, Christianity and Judaism and to the ancient Persian (Iranian) faith called Zoroastrianism.

Jewish and Christian Beliefs and Culture

At first glance Islam appears fairly similar to Christianity and Judaism. For a start, all three religions teach that there is only one God. Many of the stories and people from the Bible also appear in the Quran. The Quran also deals with some similar themes such as creation, hell and the End Times. However, when these stories and themes are looked at more closely it is clear that they are very different from the Bible.

This is especially true of what the Quran says about Jesus. In the Quran, Jesus is only a man, He is not God. The Quran says He did not die on a cross. So this is the opposite of what the Bible teaches.

Some scholars believe that a lot of the Quran is based on heretical Christian books and some devotional Christian books in the Syriac (Aramaic) language as well as wrong stories about Jesus which people were spreading at the time of Muhammad. Christian influence shows also in the design of mosques, which look like Middle Eastern churches at that time, with a dome and a tall tower.

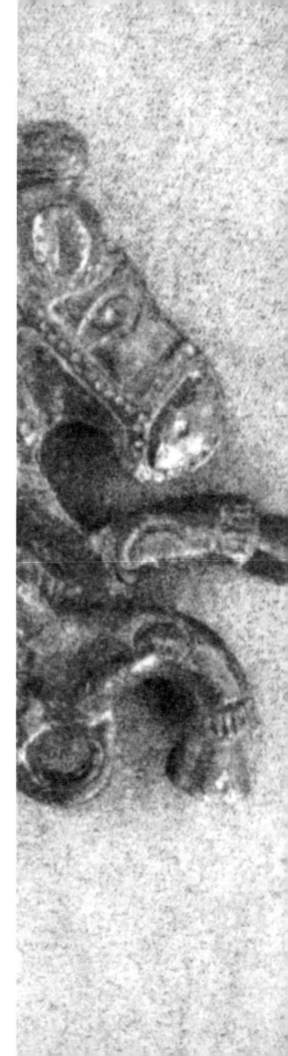

Zoroastrian Sources

Some parts of the Quran seem to have come from Zoroastrian sources; for example, the parts which describe Muhammad's visit into heaven, paradise and the black-eyed virgins, and the narrow bridge which Muslims must try to cross on the Day of Judgement. Also, many Muslims use the crescent moon as a symbol of Islam, sometimes with a star. They often appear on Muslim flags, books and mosques. Scholars think that these symbols are borrowed from the Zoroastrian Persian Empire.

Influence of Paganism

The Quran is written in a kind of ancient Arabic rhyming style similar to that used by the pagan Arab fortune-tellers.

The Arab pagans worshipped sacred stones, spirits, and many gods. It is strange that Muhammad told his followers that there was only one god but continued to use many practices and beliefs of the pagans.

As we saw in the last chapter, Muslims believe that their faith is based on five main duties or pillars. These are Declaring the Faith; Praying; Fasting during Ramadan; Giving; Hajj (pilgrimage to Mecca). It is very interesting to examine where these duties or rituals come from. While prayer and fasting followed Christian and Jewish practices, the pilgrimage came directly from the pagan religion as practiced in Mecca during Muhammad's time.

Pilgrimage to Mecca

Muslims have to try and visit Mecca at least once in their lives. This pilgrimage to Mecca is called the hajj. They have to wear special white robes and walk around the Kaaba seven times calling out the various Muslim names for God. The hajj and Mecca are very important aspects of the Islamic religion. Muhammad claimed that all the aspects of the hajj were direct revelations from God. A number of things were obviously borrowed from the pagans living in the area at the time.

Muslims say that the Kaaba was first built by Adam and then it was destroyed by the flood and then Abraham rebuilt it. However, historians agree that

Iranian painting of Adam and Eve

the Kaaba was built as a stone and wood building only a few decades before Muhammad's birth. Before that it was only a kind of open booth made of branches where the pagans used to worship and sacrifice. Muhammad's pagan tribe and pagans from all round the region used the Kaaba as the centre of their worship and sacrifices.

When Muhammad was establishing Islam he had said that Jerusalem should be the focus of Muslim prayer. However after he was rejected by the Jews and the Christians he turned his attention to Mecca. He conquered Mecca through force or through threat of overwhelming force. He turned Mecca and the Kaaba into the centre of Muslim worship so as to win support from the conquered pagan Meccans and make it easier for them to convert to Islam. Muhammad also allowed some of the other pagan practices to be included within Islam.

Muslims still sacrifice animals at Mina, and still stand at Arafat and run between two mountains in Mecca as the pagans did. The pagans used to offer sacrifices to their many gods and smear the blood on the statues of their idols. Pagans from all over the region made pilgrimages to the Kaaba. They had to walk around the Kaaba calling out the names of their gods. They also had to kiss or touch the Black Stone. All of these pagan traditions have been included into Islam except the worship of many gods.

Muslims touching the Black Stone

Read 2 Corinthians 6: 14-18.
In these verses God is telling us that we must not get involved with what unbelievers worship. We must still love them and share the Good News with them but we must be very careful not to be influenced by their beliefs. It is very clear in the Bible that God hates anything that is not holy. He wants to protect us from evil and false beliefs. These things are from the devil and they lead to pain, unhappiness or even death. This is why God tells us that we are not to have anything to do with idols, pagan worship or anything else that is not from Him. God reminds us that He is our Father and we are His children. He loves us and we must love Him and worship Him only.

Some questions to think about or discuss

- What were the main religions in Arabia during Muhammad's time?

  ....

  ....

- Who or what did Arabian pagans worship?

  ....

  ....

- What parts of the Jewish and Christian faiths did Islam borrow?

  ....

  ....

- How is what the Quran teaches about Jesus different from what the Bible teaches?

  ....

  ....

- Where does the Muslim symbol of the crescent come from?

  ....

  ....

- What are the main similarities between the Islamic pillar of pilgrimage to Mecca and paganism?

  ....

  ....

- What are the main similarities between the Islamic pillar of fasting and paganism?

  ....

  ....

- Read 2 Corinthians 6: 14-18.   What do you think "do not be yoked with unbelievers" means?

  ....

  ....

- Why do you think God tells us not to get involved with unholy things?

  ....

  ....

7

Differences
within Islam

There are many divisions within Islam, and some groups even persecute or go to war against each other. The two main divisions are Sunni Islam and Shia Islam.

The division between Sunni and Shia came about 25 years after Muhammad's death. This early period of Islam was a time of great violence. After the assassination of Caliph Uthman in 656, there was a great argument between the early Muslims as to who should take his place. The argument focused on who could take Muhammad's role as leader of the Muslims. Some claimed that Muhammad had chosen Ali, his cousin and son-in-law (husband of Muhammad's daughter Fatima), to be his successor. Others thought that it could be anyone from Muhammad's tribe (the Quraish) who was elected by the community elders.

Sunni Islam

Those Muslims who did not follow Ali and his descendants became known as Sunni Muslims. Sunni empires have dominated most of the Muslim world throughout history. Almost 90% of Muslims today are Sunnis. They believe that their leader should come from Muhammad's tribe but he does not have to be a direct descendant of Muhammad. Sunnis believe that sharia can never be changed.

Shia Islam

Those who followed Ali became called Shia Muslims. They believe that only Ali and Fatima's male descendants can be the rulers of the Muslim world (imams). One of Ali's sons, Hussein, was killed in battle. Many Shia Muslims travel to his shrine every year and remember his martyrdom with mourning and self-flagellation (whipping themselves).

Today Shias form the majority in Iran, Iraq, Azerbaijan and Bahrain. There are also large Shia minorities in Turkey, Yemen, Lebanon, Pakistan, Afghanistan

Self-flagellation by Shia Muslims

and India. Shia Muslims believe that their imams (their first spiritual leaders) were sinless and what they said or did cannot be questioned. Today they have no imam because they are waiting for one who disappeared in 832 to come back again. Shia Islam is divided into many smaller groups.

Others

Some Muslims called Kharijis said that any Muslim could be the highest leader if they showed purity of heart. The Kharijis were very extreme and only a small, moderate sub-group of them called the Ibadis still exist today. They are found in East Africa, North Africa and Oman.

Sufism (Islamic Mysticism)

Sufis are the mystics of Islam who come from a wide range of backgrounds, and can be Sunnis or Shias.

Sufis desire a personal, loving relationship with God. They long to feel close to Him. They try and achieve this through fasting, prayer, chanting God's names over and over, and meditation. They hope by chanting to enter into a trance and experience God.   Some Sufis also spin around very quickly in a dance to try and enter into a trance.

Sufis often follow spiritual leaders or "saints" (also called sheikhs, walis or pirs) who can be dead or alive. Within Sufism even women can become saints. Sufi Muslims sometimes go on long pilgrimages to the shrines of dead saints. And even though the saint is dead they try and ask for help with health and family problems. Saints are seen as protectors from evil, and sources of supernatural power. People visit the shrines of saints to ask for help in the problems of daily life, for healing, and for spiritual protection.

Sufis are great missionaries. They are responsible for bringing Islam to parts of Central Asia, south-east Asia and Africa. Many Westerners who convert to Islam do so because of Sufism.

Sufism appears to be quite peaceful but Sufis can be involved in jihad and jihad movements. They were active in the Ottoman armies in the Balkans and they actively resisted European colonialism in Senegal, Libya, Nigeria and North Africa.

Folk Islam

Folk Islam is a combination of Islam and traditional local beliefs (for example African tribal religions). It is widespread among the poor but influences all levels of Muslim society. Some Sufi marabouts in North and West Africa are very involved in Folk Islam.

Folk Islam is dominated by fear of evil spirits and powers. It includes witchcraft, sorcery, spells, charms and curses. People tie charms to their clothes or put them in their houses or cars to protect themselves. Some Folk Muslims even worship their ancestors or spirits. They also visit fortune tellers and sorcerors for help with love troubles, heath problems, demon possession, to break a curse or even put a curse on someone else.

Progressive (Modernist or Liberal) Islam

Some Muslims believe that parts of Islam should be changed to become more modern. They want the Islamic religion to be separate from the government of any country. They believe in human rights and equality of everyone, men and women, Muslims and non-Muslims. Many believe that everyone has the right to choose their religion.

These views are not very popular among Muslims. In Muslim countries progressive Muslims are often imprisoned or threatened with violence or death, so many have fled to the West.

Traditional Islam

The majority of Muslims are traditionalists. They hold on very firmly to Muslim culture and tradition. Even though sharia was formed in medieval times and it goes against many human rights they believe that it should not be changed. They believe that anything that is not part of their religion and culture is evil, especially anything that comes from the West.

Radical Islam (Islamism)

In the last 50 years a movement has arisen to restore Islam to the strength of its glory days. Radical Muslims look back to the time when many non-Muslim countries had been conquered and were

Christians who come into contact with Folk Islam must make sure that they are covered by prayer and also pray very hard for those who are trapped by Folk Islam, which is a very real and evil spiritual force.

Whirling dervishes in Turkey perform a Sufi ritual Members of Sufi groups (sometimes called orders or brotherhoods) in North and West Africa, and especially their leaders, are often called marabouts. Some orders active in Africa include the Tijaniyya, the Qadiriyya, the Shadhiliyya, the Mouridiyya and the Sammaniyya

under Islamic rule. They believe that Islam needs to purify itself, return to its roots, and regain its power. Their aim is for every country in the world to be Muslim and under sharia law. In non-Muslim states, they set up Islamic organisations at all levels of society and try to gain political influence.

The more violent radicals try and spread Islam through jihad, using terrorism, violence and coups. They threaten violence against governments in Muslim countries if they do not think they are truly Islamic.

Others spread Islam through mission (or dawa), in non-Muslim states, they set up Islamic organisations at all levels of society and try to gain political influence. They preach and seek converts and try to strengthen the influence of Islam in all areas. Some hand out food, money or aid to people only if they convert to Islam. Dawa is linked to jihad, as both have the same aim: to spread Islam and Islamic rule. All means must be used to achieve this goal. When peaceful dawa fails, violent jihad may be used.

Read Ephesians 4: 1-16.
We may look at Islam and comment about how much division there is. However, when we look at the Church today there is much division there too. Paul in Ephesians pleads for unity. Working together as Christians is God's purpose for us. We all belong to the same body. We are different parts of that same body and we have different functions. Jesus says in Matthew 12:25 that a house divided against itself cannot stand. Paul in Ephesians warns that if we are not unified as a body then we will "tossed around by the waves and blown here and there by every wind of teaching and by the cunning and craftiness of men and their deceitful scheming". As Christians, we must work together. Just as it says in Ephesians, "be completely humble and gentle; be patient, bearing with one another in love. Make every effort to keep the unity of the Spirit through the bond of peace".

Some questions to think about or discuss

• Before this session did you think that Islam was as divided as it is?

....

....

• What are the two main divisions in Islam?

....

....

- When did these two divisions separate from each other?

  ....

  ....

- Which Islamic leader and his male descendants do Shia Muslims follow?

  ....

  ....

- What are the main differences between Sunni and Shia Islam?

  ....

  ....

- What is Sufism?

  ....

  ....

- Why do you think God tells us not to get involved with unholy things?

  ....

  ....

- What do Sufis do to try and get closer to God?

  ....

  ....

- Who else do Sufis try and get help from?

  ....

  ....

- Are Sufis peaceful?

  ....

  ....

- What is Folk Islam?

  ....

  ....

- Have you ever come across Folk Islam? What is important for Christians who come into contact with Folk Islam to remember?

  ....

  ....

- What do Progressive Muslims try to do?

  ....

  ....

- What do Traditional Muslims believe?

  ....

  ....

- What do Radical Muslims want to see happen to the world?

  ....

  ....

- How are they doing this today?

  ....

  ....

- What is dawa?

  ....

  ....

- What methods do Muslims use for dawa?

  ....

  ....

- Read Ephesians 2: 1-16. Why do you think Paul tells us that as the Body of Christ we need to be unified?

  ....

  ....

- What false teachings and schemes are Christians in danger of today?

  ....

  ....

- How can we become more unified as the Body of Christ?

  ....

  ....

8

The Quran

The Quran is the Muslims' most sacred book. Muslims believe that the Quran is God's final message or revelation. It was given to Muhammad who is often called "the messenger of God" by Muslims. Muhammad said he had visits from a heavenly being who brought him the message piece by piece. Muslims believe this was the angel Gabriel. The first time this happened was in a cave when Muhammad was 40. Muslims believe that the whole message of the Quran was gradually given to Muhammad during the last 23 years of his life.

Muhammad repeated each new message from God to his followers. They memorised what he said or wrote it down on various things such as leather, camel bone, stone, leaves, wood or even tree bark.

No one collected all his messages into a single book until long after his death.

How the Quran became a Book

During his life Muhammad conquered a part of Arabia, and after his death all of Arabia was conquered and Islam spread even further into Asia and North Africa. The pieces of the Quran which had been kept in people's minds or written down were also spread across this vast area. They had been copied and repeated many times over by different followers. It is no surprise that very different versions started to appear.

The word Quran means to read or to recite

Kufic script

When Uthman, one of Muhammad's closest followers, became caliph (leader of the Muslim community), he decided to collect all the messages and put them into one book and make an official version. This happened between 650 and 656 AD.

Once the official book had been written Uthman ordered that all other versions or bits of messages (on the bones and leaves) should be destroyed.

Uthman then distributed this book as the only version that should be used. This version was written in the Arabic language using an early type of writing called Kufic script. Kufic script does not have vowels and it has no punctuation.

This made it very difficult to read, interpret or understand. Muslim scholars have argued over the true meaning for centuries.

What Muslims believe about the Quran

Muslims believe that the Quran is an exact copy, word for word, of a Quran which has existed for ever. They revere it greatly and consider that the physical book holds power. For them the book is holy, so it is very important to remember to be sensitive when speaking to Muslims about the Quran.

Muslims are often shocked by how Christians treat their Bibles. A Muslim would never carry the Quran below their waist or place it on the ground. In Muslim homes there is a special place set aside for the Quran. Muslims never write in a Quran or underline sections.

Understanding the Quran

Muslims believe that the original Quran is written in Arabic. So, only Qurans written in Arabic are considered to be true Qurans. Qurans translated into any other language are not considered true Qurans. Many Muslims all over the world memorise sections of the Quran in Arabic even if they don't speak the language or understand what they are saying.

The Quran is written in poetic form. Muslims say that reciting or chanting the Quran in Arabic has a pleasing or even hypnotic effect on them.

The Quran is made up of 114 chapters called suras. These are arranged in length order (longest to shortest, except for sura 1), not in the order they were received by Muhammad. For example, the first message that Muhammad received is actually recorded in sura 96. This is another reason why the Quran is very hard to understand.

The Quran was supposedly given to provide guidance for Muhammad and his followers for situations they were facing. This makes it difficult to understand in other situations. This is why Muslims often rely on teachers and scholars to interpret the Quran for them. These teachers and scholars can interpret the same passage in very different ways.

There are also a number of contradictions in the Quran. Most Muslims explain these contradictions by saying that later revelations to Muhammad cancel out the earlier ones. This is known as "abrogation". This helps a Muslim understand which part of the Quran they should obey.

But there are problems with this approach. Firstly Muslim scholars argue over which parts of the Quran came first and which parts came later. Secondly, as the years passed Muhammad became less tolerant and more warlike. This means that the peaceful parts of the Quran which were written during Muhammad's earlier and tolerant years are cancelled out by the violent verses of his later years. So when people quote peaceful verses from the Quran, many Muslims would not consider these verses relevant any more.

Contents of the Quran

The Quran includes stories about people in the Bible such as Abraham, Moses, Joseph and Jesus. It describes the End Times, the Day of Judgement, paradise and hell. However, the stories and descriptions in the Quran differ a lot from those found in the Bible. The Quran also has rules about marriage, divorce, inheritance, food, slavery, war and many other things.

What the Quran says about:

The Old and New Testaments

The Old and New Testaments are mentioned more than 120 times in the Quran.

The Quran teaches that the Bible is the genuine word of God. However, Muslims claim that the Jews and Christians have changed their scriptures from what God originally gave them, so many of them do not have much respect for the Bible.   It is important for Christians to know that there is much more historical evidence to support the validity of the Bible than for the Quran.

Jesus Christ

Jesus is called Isa in the Quran. Muslims believe that He was a prophet, was born of a virgin, performed miracles and was sinless. However, the Quran clearly says that Jesus did not die on the cross. It denies that God has a Son. And most important the Quran claims that Jesus is not God. This is one of the most important differences between Islam and Christianity.

Muslims treat their Qurans with great respect. They keep them on a high shelf, carefully wrapped. They do not put them on the ground, or write in them, or hold them below waist-level. They would be angry if they saw anyone doing that to their holy book

Read John 1: 1-18.
As Christians we believe that Jesus is the Word of God.   The power of the Bible is in the truth of the words. For Christians, true power lies in the living Word who is Jesus Christ, our Lord and Saviour, and in His shed blood.

Some questions to think about or discuss

- What did you know or understand about the Quran before this session?

  ....

  ....

- What did you find interesting about what you have just learnt?

  ....

  ....

- Why do you think it is important for us to be sensitive when talking to Muslims about the Quran?

  ....

  ....

- What things should you be careful not to do or say about the Quran?

  ....

  ....

- What do you think about the paper and ink of the Quran holding power?

  ....

  ....

- Why is the Quran difficult for even Muslims to understand?

  ....

  ....

- How does the Quran's teaching about Jesus differ from what Christians believe?

  ....

  ....

- Read John 1: 1-18. Who do we believe is the Word of God?

  ....

  ....

- How is this different from what Muslims believe?

  ....

  ....

9

Muslim Traditions & Law

The Sunna

Muslims believe that everything that Muhammad did and said was directed by God. Muslims believe that they have to follow Muhammad's example. Muhammad's way of life, his actions and his words are called his sunna. When Muslims say that they are following Muhammad's sunna, they mean that they are trying to be like Muhammad.

The Hadith

What Muhammad did and said was passed on by word of mouth for many generations. It was not until 150 years after his death that Muslim scholars started to gather together some of these stories and write them down. Each scholar made his own collection of stories. These collections are called the hadith. They wrote down a long list of who had passed on the story from one to another down the years. Some of these stories or traditions of Muhammad are considered more reliable than others. The Sunni Muslims have different stories or traditions about Muhammad from the Shia Muslims.

The hadith is very important to Muslims as a source of guidance from God; the only thing considered more important is the Quran. The hadith is often easier to understand than the Quran so Muslims often refer to it more than the Quran. Muslim scholars use the hadith to explain the Quran's meaning and make legal rulings. The hadith helps Muslims know how they should live their lives. Much of Islamic law and culture is found in the writings of the hadith rather than the Quran. For example, the Quran tells Muslims to pray, but it is from the hadith that Muslims know how often to pray, what time of day to pray and how to pray.

Sharia

Islam is not just a religion but also a legal system. These laws are called the sharia and come from the Quran and the hadith. The sharia tells Muslims what they can do or what is allowed (halal) and what they can't do or what is forbidden (haram). There are four versions of sharia in Sunni Islam and other versions in Shia Islam. They all have slightly different laws. In Europe all the different versions are used as Muslims have migrated to Europe from many different countries. In France the Maliki version is important because most Muslims there originate from North Africa. In the UK the Hanafi version is important because most British Muslims originate from Pakistan and Bangladesh.

Every part of a Muslim's life is affected by sharia – what to eat, marriage, treatment of women, education, business, medicine, inheritance, war and worship. Muslims often say that sharia was quite fair compared to many cultures during the early history of Islam. However, it has not changed for more than twelve centuries and is considered very harsh by modern standards. Many people say that sharia goes against basic human rights and religious freedom. For example, there is a death penalty for adultery or if someone converts from Islam to another religion. If someone steals then their hand should be chopped off and if someone is caught drinking alcohol they are whipped.

In most Muslim countries parts of sharia are used in the legal system or influences it. In non-Muslim countries sharia is sometimes imposed by Muslim leaders on to the minority Muslim community that is living there. In Western countries Muslims often try to get parts of sharia inserted into the main legal system and other aspects of public life. Because sharia is so different from most countries' legal systems this sometimes causes problems between the state, the non-Muslim majority and the Muslim minority.

Sharia and Non-Muslims

The Muslim communities living in many non-Muslim countries are putting heavy pressure on governments to add parts of sharia law to their legal

A halal restaurant

systems. Some countries have given in to these pressures and non-Muslim majorities are allowing their Muslim minorities to live to some extent by a different legal system. Countries where this has happened include Canada, the UK, Germany, Kenya, Uganda, and South Africa. In some countries like Nigeria, certain states or provinces that have a Muslim majority are governed mainly by sharia law.

In Muslim countries, there are sometimes laws which make life more difficult for non-Muslims. Even if there are no laws, the police and judges and ordinary people often treat non-Muslims badly and no one stops them from doing so. Christian and Jewish communities are often despised and persecuted. They may find it hard to get examination passes, get a job, or get a promotion or are treated unfairly by the police or courts. Non-Muslims are treated as second-class citizens. It is difficult to get permits to build new churches, and even repairing old churches may cause trouble. In some Muslim countries no public Christian worship is allowed. Converts from Islam to Christianity in Muslim countries usually have to meet together in secret to worship. Muslim groups complain that their human rights are violated if sharia is not introduced into non-Muslim countries; yet in Muslim countries they violate the human rights of Christians and other non-Muslims through persecution and discrimination.

Taqiyya

Taqiyya means to deceive or to lie. This is allowed in Islam for several reasons. Taqiyya was first used by early Muslims when their lives were in danger. They could lie to save their lives. Later it became acceptable to lie or deceive to protect not just life but also property and honour. Even later, what was supposed to be just for emergencies became normal practice. Taqiyya is especially permitted if it is for the good of Muslims and of Islam. It is now very much part of Islamic culture.

The Quran says that lying is allowed. The hadith explains three situations where Muslims can lie:

- a man may lie to his wife to please her
- to bring peace between two groups that have been quarrelling
- in war

The last reason – war – is often used by Muslims today to mean anything that will spread Islam or help or protect Islam or Muslims. In other words, Muslims feel that it is okay to lie to non-Muslims about things like: Islam; its history; their plans to spread Islam. The lies often include the statements that Islam is a religion of peace and that Muslims treat all people of all faiths fairly. Muslims are also in the process of rewriting their history to make it seem that they have always been the victims and make Islam look more peaceful or tolerant.

The End Times in Islam

The hadith say much about the End Times and the Day of Judgement. First there will be famines, earthquakes, wars, immorality and unbelief. An Antichrist (Dajjal) will appear and cause corruption and oppression all over the world. He will deceive many by his miracles and false teachings. He will be helped by the Jews. A saviour, the Mahdi, will appear to fight the Dajjal, Jews and Christians and restore Islam to its original glory.

Jesus returns to earth as a Muslim and helps the Mahdi defeat the Dajjal. Jesus breaks the cross; kills all pigs, and converts all Christians to Islam. All Jews are killed and no non-Muslims are left. The Mahdi sets up an Islamic world kingdom of justice, peace and prosperity with Jerusalem as his capital. There is a terrible final battle against Gog and Magog, but the Muslims win with the help of Jesus. Jesus reigns with the Mahdi for 40 years, marries, has children, then dies and is buried as a Muslim next to Muhammad. Finally the Mahdi dies too.

Then there are new signs of the End as the sun rises in the West. A terrible Beast comes from the earth and the Kaaba is destroyed.

Finally the Day of Judgement comes. Every person's good and evil deeds are weighed in the scales to decide whether they go to paradise or hell. All non-Muslims will go to hell. Even most Muslims will have to spend some time in hell before going to paradise. The Quran describes paradise as a garden, full of wonderful fruits, rivers of wine, honey and milk, beautiful girls and boys, and seemingly much sexual activity. Hell is a place of torment.

Read Romans 7: 4-6.
As Christians Jesus Christ died to set us free from sin and from the law. This means that when we accept Jesus as our Saviour our sins are immediately forgiven and we receive eternal life. We do not have to worry that sin will lead to death any more. However, by accepting Christ into our lives we are called to live holy lives. We can never be perfect or sinless on our own. But when we have Christ and the Holy Spirit in our lives we begin to find out that He helps us become more like Him. Our lives start to show this. Sinful things we wanted to do before no longer interest us. We start to live according to the Spirit.

Some questions to think about or discuss

- From what you have just learnt how do Muslims view Muhammad and what he said and did?

  ....
  ....

- What is the Sunna?

  ....
  ....

- What do you think about Muslims following the example of Muhammad without question?

  ....
  ....

- When were all of the things that Muhammad did and said collected and written down?

  ....
  ....

- What are these written records called?

  ....
  ....

- Why should we question their reliability?

  ....
  ....

- What is sharia?

  ....
  ....

- Do you think that sharia is relevant in today's society?

  ....
  ....

- What do you think of sharia being part of a non-Muslim country's legal system?

  ....

  ....

- According to sharia what would happen to a Muslim if they decided to become a Christian?

  ....

  ....

- How are Christians living in Muslim countries usually treated?

  ....

  ....

- What is taqiyya?

  ....

  ....

- At first Muslims were allowed to lie in emergencies. Why do you think that they lie now?

  ....

  ....

- What do Muslims believe will happen in the End Times?

  ....

  ....

- What do Muslims believe paradise is like?

  ....

  ....

- Read Romans 7: 4-6. As Christians why do you think Christ died for us?

  ....

  ....

- We are called to live holy lives. How do we do this if we as humans and are sinful by nature?

  ....

  ....

- How does our understanding of the law and grace differ from a Muslim understanding of law?

  ....

  ....

10

Muslim Culture & Worldview

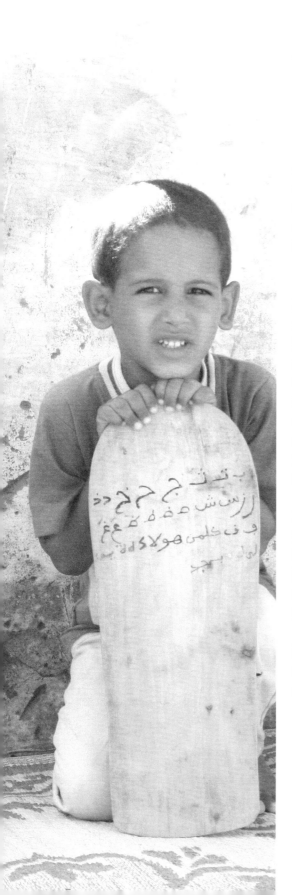

Islam is a very diverse religion. Muslims in different countries and regions have different cultures and customs. However, there are some things that stay the same in most Muslim societies. The cultures, customs and worldview mentioned below are just parts of a wider Islamic culture.

Islam as a Way of Life

Islam affects all parts of life. It is more than just a religion. It is a way of life. All aspects of a Muslim's life are meant to be influenced by Islam. Islam and sharia govern what Muslims are allowed to eat, how they are educated, how they treat women and non-Muslims, how they bank their money, how they dress etc. Even everyday language is full of religious expressions. Many Muslims who do not consider themselves to be very religious still follow many of the Islamic customs as part of their Islamic culture.

Islam is seen as a religion, a civilisation, a nationality, a culture, and an identity. Muslims feel that they belong to a wider "Islamic nation". It is important for Muslims to identify themselves to each other and to the non-Muslim world by how they dress and speak and conduct their rituals.

Many Muslims do not believe that government and religion can be separate. They also feel that the law of a country should be based on Islamic law, sharia.

Honour and Shame

One of the most important values in Muslim culture is honour. Honour is based on how others see you, not on how you really are. It is important that others think that you are generous, follow the Five Pillars of Islam, have an obedient, modest wife and obedient children, and have avenged any insults to your family or to Islam.

A Muslim would see any criticism as a personal insult. It is especially shameful for a Muslim to be criticised in front of others.

Many Muslims believe that a person's honour, dignity and reputation are the most important things in their lives. Sometimes honour is more important than logic, facts or even life itself. Many Muslims believe that if honour is lost it must be avenged at all costs otherwise they will remain dishonoured forever. This is why some Muslims will kill people they love rather than let the family be disgraced. For example it is a huge disgrace for a Muslim woman to refuse to marry her arranged husband. If she runs away to avoid the marriage her family may find and kill her to punish her and avenge the shame that they have suffered by her disobedience.

Family honour is very much based on the behaviour of its women, who must dress and behave modestly. This is why women are so heavily controlled by Muslim men. Any disobedience must be severely punished to save honour.

Having a family member convert from Islam to Christianity (or any other religion) brings the greatest possible shame on a family. The convert is seen as a traitor to the umma (Islamic nation). Many converts all over the world are killed by their families to restore honour.

Constant Fear

Most Muslims do not believe in a personal, loving and faithful God who will protect and care for them. For them God is distant and unpredictable. They cannot rely on him and so they live in constant fear. Many Muslims are very fatalistic and do not think that they have any control over their lives. They fear death, evil spirits, shame, hell, curses and catastrophes.

Waiting in line for vaccination

Blaming Non-Muslims

Many Muslims claim that non-Muslims everywhere in the world are plotting to humiliate, dominate, exploit, and manipulate them. They blame non-Muslims for all troubles that Muslims face. While they are often quick to insult other religions and cultures, at the same time Muslims are extremely sensitive about Islam. They demand compensation for any real or imagined insults to Islam. Muslims believe that Islam deserves special treatment and protection. For example Muslims still demand compensation and apologies from the West for the Crusades even though they happened centuries ago, and it was the Muslims who were the original aggressors, and the Muslims who eventually won.

This attitude has come from the early history of Islam, when Muhammad and his followers were often rejected by the people they were trying to reach. This made the early Muslims feel like victims and they did not trust anyone who was not a Muslim. Aggressive mistrust of non-Muslims has carried over for generations. Certain passages of the Quran and hadith are used to teach Muslims to have a victim mentality from an early age.

Islamic Nation or Umma

Muslims believe that they belong to a global Islamic nation made of all the Muslims in the world. This is called the umma. Many Muslims feel greater loyalty to the umma than to their own country. It is the duty of Muslims to defend the umma from outsiders at all costs, including by jihad. This is why many young Muslim men from Western countries get involved in various conflicts across the world, for example, Iraq, Afghanistan, Chechnya and Sudan.

Muslims Revere Muhammad Greatly

Muslims believe they have to follow Muhammad's example and commands without question. Whenever they refer to Muhammad they say "may Allah bless him and grant him peace". Although Muslims acknowledge that Muhammad is just a man they respect and revere him almost as if he was God. They feel any disrespect of Muhammad is as bad as blasphemy. In Pakistan there is a law which has the death penalty for anyone who disrespects Muhammad.

Muslims believe that if non-Muslims disrespect Muhammad it is their duty to defend him. This is sometimes done through violence, riots, threats or terrorism. For example, a Danish newspaper published some cartoons of Muhammad in 2005. The Islamic community all around the world protested strongly. Some Muslim leaders used this event to incite hatred and violence against Western targets and against Christian minorities in Muslim countries. Many people were injured or even killed. Many Islamic newspapers all over the world feel free to publish very insulting articles, pictures and cartoons of Christ, Christians and Jews and yet some Muslims react violently when they believe Islam has been insulted.

Muslims protesting about the Danish cartoons, Amsterdam

Read Colossians 3: 12-17.
Muslims believe that they belong to one global community or nation of Islam, the umma. However, as we have learnt, there is a lot of fear, deceit, disunity and violence within Muslim culture. The Bible teaches us that, as Christians, we are part of the Body of Christ and we are His family. The Body of Christ is very different from the Islamic nation or umma. God calls us to peace. God teaches us to be holy, compassionate, kind, humble and forgiving. God tells us that His Body is held together by a single factor and that is love.

Some questions to think about or discuss

- How much of a Muslim's life is governed by sharia?

  ....
  ....

- What do you think the phrase "Islam is more than a religion" means?

  ....
  ....

- What do you think the dangers are of not separating religion and government?

  ....
  ....

- In what ways can a Muslim lose their honour?

  ....
  ....

- What is the greatest shame for a Muslim family and how is this sometimes dealt with?

  ....

  ....

- What types of things do Muslims fear?

  ....

  ....

- How do you think living under constant fear could affect the lives of Muslims?

  ....

  ....

- Who or what do Muslims often blame their troubles on?

  ....

  ....

- From your experience do you think that Muslims live in a victim culture?

  ....

  ....

- What does the umma mean?

  ....

  ....

- If the umma is under threat what do Muslims have to do?

  ....

  ....

- How do Muslims react to any disrespect of Muhammad?

  ....

  ....

- Read Colossians 3: 12-17. From what you just learnt how does the Islamic nation differ from the Body of Christ?

  ....

  ....

11

Women
in Islam

A Woman's Place in the Family

A woman's place is in the home. Her role is to produce sons for her husband, care for them and to do housework.

A woman is always under the protection and control of a male relative. This could be her father, husband, brother, uncle or son. The honour of the family depends greatly on the women and girls being obedient and modest. It is very important that a girl is a virgin at marriage.

In a strict family a woman must get permission from a male relative even to visit her mother or sisters. And if she was allowed to visit she would not be allowed to go on her own. A woman would never be allowed to talk to or touch a man unless he was a close relative. For example, it would cause great offence if an unknown man greeted a Muslim woman with a handshake. On social occasions women and men normally gather in different rooms.

The reason why women must be under male guardianship and control is that they are seen as lacking in intelligence, morals and religion. They are also seen as a source of sexual temptation to men. Muhammad said that most of the people in hell are women.

Clothing

A Muslim woman must be covered from neck to ankle, including her arms up to her wrists. Her hair must also be covered. The clothes must be very loose fitting. In some cultures a woman must also cover her face, hands and feet.

A scarf which covers the hair and neck is called a hijab

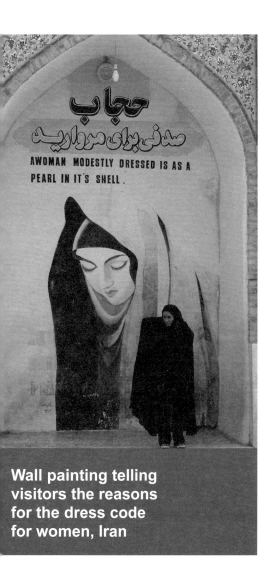

AWOMAN MODESTLY DRESSED IS AS A PEARL IN IT'S SHELL.

Wall painting telling visitors the reasons for the dress code for women, Iran

In some Muslim communities a woman must wear a burqa covering her from head to toe, whenever she is outside of the home.

When Christian women visit with Muslims it is important for them to remember to dress modestly.

Legal Status of Women

In Islam women are considered inferior to men. They have very few rights and freedoms. They are often treated very harshly. Islamic law (sharia) only gives women half the value of men. For example, in a sharia court case two female witnesses equal one male witness. Also a woman would inherit only half of what her brother does. When compensation is given, a woman gets half what a man gets for the same injury.

Marriage

In Islam marriage is seen as a God-given duty. It is not good to be single. Many Muslims think that if an older person is still single it must be because they are sinful. Marriage is also seen as a legal contract – the man pays the dowry for exclusive rights to the woman's body.

Muslims usually see marriage as a way of joining two families together rather than just two people. Because of this almost all Muslim marriages are arranged, and the young people have little or no say in the choice. Some couples do not meet each other until the wedding day. Love is expected to follow later, as they get to know each other. A young person is allowed to refuse their arranged marriage partner. However, to do so would bring such shame and disgrace to the family that this hardly ever happens.

It is also very common for Muslims to marry close relatives, for example first or second cousins. If a marriage is arranged outside the family, then the financial and social status of the families will be important factors to consider.

A Muslim man is allowed to have up to four wives at the same time. Having more than one wife is called polygamy. He is required to treat all his wives the same. He is allowed to beat them if they are disobedient.

Muhammad is seen as the perfect example in Islam. Muhammad married a six-year-old girl and consummated the marriage when she was nine. Following this example sharia permits the marriage of young girls.

Treatment of Christian and other Non-Muslim Women

A Muslim man is allowed to marry a Christian woman. In fact this is very much encouraged as a way of spreading Islam in Africa and many other parts of the world. Muslim men are sometimes given money as a reward for marrying Christian women. They are paid for every Christian woman that they marry and more if she is a pastor's daughter. Often the wife is expected to convert to Islam. Any children born from such a marriage are considered Muslim. A Muslim woman is not allowed to marry a Christian or other non-Muslim man.

Because all the children of a Muslim man are considered Muslims, many Muslim men will try and have as many children as they can. This has been one of the ways Muslims have spread Islam across the world. Some Muslim men think it is all right to rape Christian and other non-Muslim women, seeing it almost like jihad. Muslims think that rape brings dishonour to the Christians and that any children that are born because of the rape are Muslim.

Divorce

It is a terrible disgrace for an unhappy or abused Muslim wife to leave her husband. To avoid shame and dishonour, her family will do all they can to make her rejoin her husband. Honour is more important than happiness no matter how badly a wife has been treated by her husband or in-laws. Muslim women are often trapped in very abusive and violent marriages.

According to sharia, it is very easy for a Muslim man to divorce his wife. All he needs to do is say to her three times and in front of a witness "I divorce you". It is much harder for a Muslim woman to divorce her husband. Because it is such a disgrace for a woman to be divorced she will often be rejected by her own family and have nowhere to go. The children of a marriage belong to the husband and his family. If a couple divorce, the wife must give the children to her ex-husband. If a man dies his widow must give the children to his relatives. In some Muslim communities men are able to have temporary marriages called muta. The length of the

Entrance to a ladies' prayer room in a mosque

marriage could be from one hour to 99 years. This means that a man can sleep with a prostitute but will not be breaking any Muslim laws because she is his wife for the few hours that they are together. He then divorces her. This has been a cause of AIDS spreading in Muslim communities in many parts of Africa.

Spiritual Duties

Women have to practise the five pillars of Islam, just as men do. Very few Muslim women go to the mosque; they are encouraged to pray at home. For those that are allowed to attend mosque, they have to pray in a separate place. They are not allowed to be seen or heard by the men. The only way women can get to paradise is to obey their husbands.

Many Muslim women have little knowledge of Islam or the teaching of the Quran, though they generally know all about the Day of Judgement. Many Muslim women know the hadith that says most men will go to paradise while most of the people in hell will be women. It is not surprising that many Muslim women live in constant fear.

Read Galatians 3: 28.
The Bible teaches us that we are all equal in the sight of God. Jesus Christ died for all of us. No one has higher status than anyone else. It does not matter to God what colour you are, what country you come from or whether you are male or female. We are all heirs to the Kingdom of God. So if God treats everyone the same we should too. Women should be respected and treated as equals. Read Ephesians 5: 22-33. In Christianity men and women are equal, but Paul tells us that husbands have a spiritual headship. Christian husbands should love their wives as Christ loved the Church and gave Himself up for it.

Some questions to think about or discuss

- What is the legal status of women in Islam and how are they treated?

  ....

  ....

- How many women witnesses would equal a male witness?

  ....

  ....

- Why is a woman so well controlled and protected in a Muslim home?

  ....

  ....

- What is the woman's role in a Muslim home?

  ....

  ....

- If a woman disobeys her husband what might he do to her?

  ....

  ....

- If a woman disobeys how would it affect the family's reputation?

  ....

  ....

- If a woman disobeys what might she fear would happen after she dies?

  ....

  ....

- How must a Muslim woman dress outside of her home?

  ....

  ....

- Have you seen different ways Muslim women have dressed in your community?

  ....

  ....

- If a Christian woman meets with a Muslim community how should she dress?

  ....

  ....

- How do Muslims view marriage and singleness?

  ....

  ....

- How are Muslim men encouraged to marry Christian women?

  ....

  ....

- Why do you think that Muslim men are encouraged to marry Christian women?

  ....

  ....

- What must a man do in order to divorce women?

  ....

  ....

- What do you think about Muslim men being able to have a temporary marriage?

  ....

  ....

- Why do so many Muslim women live in fear?

  ....

  ....

- How do you feel about the way women are treated in Islam?

  ....

  ....

- Read Galatians 3:28   As Christians how do you think women should be treated?

  ....

  ....

- How does the way Muslim men treat women differ from how Christian men should treat women?

  ....

  ....

- Read Ephesians 5:22-33. How should a Christian husband treat his wife?

  ....

  ....

12

How Muslims view
Non-Muslims

The first Muslims were often despised and rejected by surrounding tribes and communities. So the early Muslims always felt that they were in danger from pagans. Some even fled to the Christian country of Abyssinia (modern day Ethiopia) where they were given safe refuge. Later when Islam became stronger it began to expand through jihad. Even though they conquered large parts of land for Islam, they were only a small group. They feared that the much larger populations in the countries that they had conquered would rise up and re-take their lands. This made them mistrust anyone who was not a Muslim and led to many laws being created to ensure that Muslims were always dominant over non-Muslims.

Types of Non-Muslims

The Quran and the hadith divide non-Muslims into three categories – "The People of the Book", pagans and apostates.

- People of the Book are those who believe in one God and also have their own scriptures. Although some Muslims include other religions, most agree that the People of the Book are Christians and Jews.

- Pagans are people who worship many gods.

- Apostates are Muslims who have left Islam to join another faith.

Treatment of Non-Muslims

As Muhammad gained support he began to conquer surrounding land and people. Conquered non-Muslims were treated in different ways depending on whether they were pagans or People of the Book. The pagans had to be wiped out by either converting them to Islam or killing them.

Muhammad believed that he was the final prophet of the Jews and Christians. He wanted them to follow him. And so he treated them differently from pagans. Jews and Christians were allowed to keep their faith and their lives as long as they submitted to Muslim rule and paid a special tax called jizya. They were still treated harshly and considered inferior to Muslims. They were called dhimmis. They were protected as long as they kept the harsh conditions imposed on them. If they rebelled against their Muslim oppressors they could be killed.

Apostates were seen as traitors. So they were killed.

Treatment of Non-Muslims Today

Just as in the early days of Islam, most Christians in Muslim countries are not treated as equal citizens. The kind of problems and pressures they face vary from country to country. But many of the restrictions they suffer are like the sharia rules for dhimmis. For example, it can be hard for Christians to get permission to build or even repair churches, they can get into trouble for noisy worship or if they do not show respect to Muslims, they may not be promoted to high positions at work. It is sad that Christians sometimes convert to Islam to escape the pressures on them in Muslim countries.

Government prejudice: In some Muslim countries it is the government that treats Christians badly through unjust laws. They have very few rights. In Saudi Arabia, for example, Christians are not allowed to show their faith in public and can even be arrested for meeting to pray in their own homes. Some governments pass laws which discriminate against Christians. In other countries, where there

Mosque minaret dominates church towers in Egypt

are no such laws, Christians may still suffer at the hands of the authorities. They can be threatened, arrested, imprisoned or tortured, sometimes to death, even without breaking any law, just because the police and judges are against them. The main targets are church leaders, evangelists and Christians who have converted from Islam.

Extremist persecution: In some Muslim-controlled areas Christians are persecuted by Muslim extremists. Although the state or community leaders do not persecute Christians themselves they do little to protect the Christians or stop the persecution. These Muslim extremists look to stir up hatred against Christians and often bring false claims against them. In areas where Muslims and Christians used to live together in peace these extremists have urged mobs to attack the Christians. This has happened in Egypt, Nigeria, Pakistan, Indonesia, Uganda and Kenya.

Community persecution: In some Muslim countries or Muslim areas Christians are treated badly by their neighbours and Muslim communities. They find it very difficult to make a living because few people will hire or trade with them because they are Christians. They are treated as second-class citizens. They are often blamed by Muslims for anything that goes wrong. This can lead to Christians being punished by mobs because Muslims think that they have caused diseases, famines and other disasters. Some Muslims even think that treating a Christian well is a sin.

These terrible things do unfortunately happen around the world. However, there are some places where Christians and Muslims live peacefully together.

Why Muslims Despise and Persecute Christians and Other Non-Muslims

The early verses in the Quran, while Muhammad was living at Mecca, were peaceful towards Jews and Christians. He said that Muslims should treat them with respect. However, when they rejected him and his message, he turned much more violent towards them. Muslims believe that the later more violent and harsh Quranic verses, which came to

Church in Iraq after bomb attack

Muhammad at Medina, cancel out the earlier more peaceful ones. This is why some Muslims are so critical of anything that is Christian or Jewish. Muslims believe that Muhammad is the final prophet but this was not acceptable to the Jews and Christians in Arabia. Muhammad therefore went on to say that Jews and Christians must have changed their scriptures, otherwise they would have accepted him.

Muslims who pray five times a day repeat the most important prayer 17 times each day. This prayer is the first sura of the Quran. It asks God not to let them be like "those who have earned God's anger" or "those who have gone astray". Many Muslims are taught that "those who have earned God's anger" refers to the Jews while "those who have gone astray" refers to Christians. If Muslims pray this prayer 17 times a day it is not surprising that they begin to despise both Jews and Christians. There are also verses in the Quran and hadith which forbid Muslims to make friends with Christians or even to greet Christians.

Many Muslims believe that all Westerners are Christians. Muslims feel that Western colonialism in the past and the "War on Terror" now are attacks by Western "Christians" on Islam. They also see Christian missions and globalisation as attempts to weaken Islam. Muslims think that every Christian in the world must be an ally of the West. They expect Christians in Muslim countries to feel more loyalty to the West than to their own country. Many Muslims are retaliating to the "War on Terror" by attacking Christians who live in Muslim countries or in Muslim areas.

Radical Muslims want a purification of Islam. They want Islam to return to its golden age when Islam was its strongest and many countries were under Islamic rule. They want Islam to expand until the whole world is under sharia and Islamic rule. They believe that if non-Muslims are not willing to submit to Islam then Muslims must wage a jihad or holy war against them to force them to convert or submit or be killed.

Converts from Islam to Christianity

One of the greatest sins in Islam is to deny the faith and convert to another religion. If someone leaves Islam they are considered by Muslims to be a traitor. According to sharia this sin of apostasy – leaving the faith – must be punished by death for men. Some versions of sharia have a death sentence for women too, and some say women must be imprisoned. There are a few countries which have the death sentence for leaving Islam, just like sharia, but it is very rarely carried out officially. However, sometimes converts disappear and are mysteriously killed, probably by the police or army. Converts can be killed by their own family for bringing shame on them. They are often thrown out of their family or job; their husband or wife and children are taken away and some are severely beaten or even killed. This is one of the main reasons why Muslims are very reluctant to convert to Christianity.

A 1978 fatwa from Egypt about a convert from Islam to Christianity: *"This man has committed apostasy; he must be given a chance to repent and if he does not then he must be killed according to Shariah"*

Read Romans 12: 9-21 and Matthew 5: 10-12.
Jesus tells us to rejoice when people persecute us because we are blessed and our reward is in heaven. God teaches us to live a life that is full of love. He tells us to not only love other Christians but to even love those who hate us, persecute us and speak evil of us. Even if people hate us we must bless them and love them. We are taught that we must be humble and live in peace with others. We must not take revenge on those who hurt us. God knows that evil cannot be beaten by other evil. Only goodness and love can beat evil and hatred.

Some questions to think about or discuss

- What are the two categories that Muslims divide non-Muslims into?

....

....

- How were each of these groups treated by Muhammad and his followers?

....

....

- How do some Muslim governments treat Christians?

  ....

  ....

- How do some Muslim extremists persecute Christians?

  ....

  ....

- What persecution could Christians face by a Muslim community?

  ....

  ....

- What are some reasons why Muslims despise and persecute Christians?

  ....

  ....

- What is an apostate and how do Muslims treat them?

  ....

  ....

- Read Romans 12: 9-21 and Matthew 5: 10-12. How does God teach us to treat those who hate or persecute us?

  ....

  ....

- How does what God teaches us in Romans 12: 9-21and Matthew 5: 10-12 differ from how Muslims treat Christians?

  ....

  ....

13

How to Witness
to Muslims

Read John 3: 16 and Matthew 28: 18-20.
We have learnt a lot about Islam and Muslims and the differences between Islam and Christianity. It is important to remember that despite these differences we must love Muslims and try our hardest to show them the way to Jesus Christ, our Lord and Saviour. It says in John 3: 16 that God so loved the world that he sent His only Son to die on the cross for our sins. Whoever believes in Him will not die but have eternal life. This means that God loves everyone in the whole world.

As Christians we are commanded to share the Good News with the whole world. Many Christians want to witness to Muslims but they are too afraid of Islam or do not know what to do. We must remember what it says in Matthew 28: 18-20. God has given us the authority and power to witness to anyone on earth. We have nothing to fear or doubt. If we pray for wisdom and guidance God will give us the opportunities to meet Muslim friends and the words to use when speaking to them.

Prayer and Discernment

Some Muslims are more serious about their faith than others. There are some very strict Muslims who are only interested in arguing against Christianity and promoting Islam. There are those whose hearts are more open and who are genuinely interested in having conversations about Christianity. And there are those who really want to know about Christ. Pray that the Lord would show you whose hearts are open. It is probably best to spend more time with those whose hearts are more open. However, if you have next door neighbours who are Muslim, whatever their heart is like, it is important to reach them with the Gospel, as the Lord has placed them across your path.

We must make sure that we are spiritually prepared for meeting Muslims. Ask the Lord to open their hearts to His Spirit. Remember your Muslim friends may be trying to convert you just as much as you are trying to convert them. Ask God to protect you from their arguments and to give you wisdom to know what to say or do that will demonstrate Christ's love. Continue to pray and intercede for them. Many Muslims even have dreams of Jesus or miraculous signs and wonders happen in their lives to help them come to know the Lord.

Friendship

Muslims are not usually won to the Lord by clever arguments against Islam. It is better to approach Muslims in a friendly and loving manner that demonstrates Christ's love.

Be genuinely interested in someone as a person rather than just a potential convert. Always remember that Muslims are ordinary human beings like us. They experience many of the same joys, sorrows, and anxieties that we do. Get to know about them as people and about their lives and culture and at the same time share about your life, about what it means to be a Christian and about your relationship with Christ. In Muslim culture men and women are often treated very differently and kept apart. It is normal in Islamic culture that men speak only to men, women speak only to women (except within the family). When with Muslims it is important to dress modestly and not to interact with the opposite sex, and especially not to touch them. Christian men should become friends with Muslim men and Christian women should become friends with Muslim women. Muslim men sometimes want to become friends with Christian women but this is often used by Muslims as a way of trying to convert Christian women to Islam. Christian women must be on their guard against this and make sure that they do not spend any time alone with Muslim men.

When building friendships it can be very easy to have only a social relationship. Many Christians do this to avoid offending their Muslim friends. You have to decide at the beginning of ministry to Muslims that you mean business with God with regard to sharing the Gospel. Once a friendship develops it becomes more and more difficult to share Christ if we have not done so from the beginning. You may say, "My life speaks of my faith", but that is not enough; you also have to speak about Christ. Sharing of our faith should come naturally. It is important to show that our faith is very important to us.

What to share

Many people say that to win Muslims to the Lord you don't have to know a lot about Islam; you just have to know a lot about Jesus.

Instead of discussing the negatives of Islam it is best to focus on the Bible and on Christ and how He died for us so that our sins may be forgiven. Talk about your relationship with the Lord. To Muslims God is very distant and very impersonal. Tell Muslims what Christ has done in your life and what He is doing in your life today. This will show Muslims that you are serious about your faith and that Jesus is a personal God and is with us every moment of the day.

If you feel that you have built enough trust with your friend, even offer to pray for things in their lives, for example their health or finances. You may be surprised at how much they would like you to pray for them. However, do not be offended if they refuse. It is a big step for a Muslim to agree to be prayed for by a Christian and it sometimes takes a long time to build enough trust for this to happen. Another way to help Muslims get to know about Jesus more is to give them a copy of a New Testament as a gift. A good place for them to start reading is Matthew or Luke.

Accepting Christ

Spend time in prayer asking God to show you the best time to ask a Muslim friend if they would like to accept Christ. Sometimes we can do this with a comment such as "Would you really like to know Jesus and not just about him?" or "Would you like to experience God in your life?" Another question you can ask is "Do you want to be sure that you will go to heaven when you die?"

Asking Muslims these questions can cause them to think hard and can bring them to the point where they can find and know God through the Lord Jesus Christ. Make sure they understand that the decision to follow Christ means that they will give up being a Muslim.

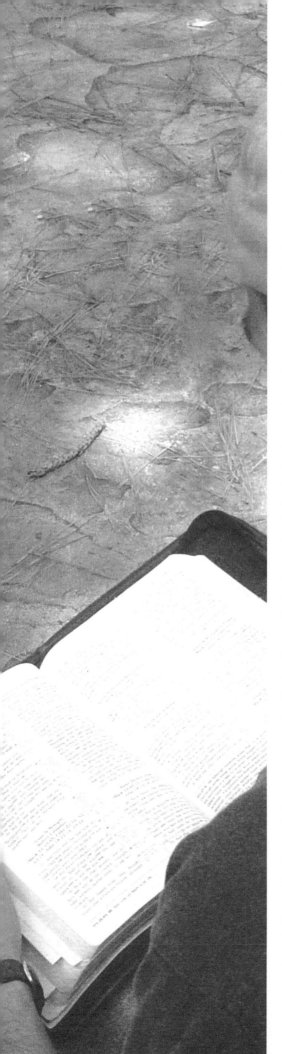

Convert Care

As Christians we must be aware of what it means for a Muslim to convert to Christianity. Leaving Islam is seen as treachery and in most instances leads to punishment from a person's family, friends, work colleagues, community or the authorities. According to Islamic law, someone who leaves Islam should be killed. In some places converts are murdered by their own family for bringing shame upon them. In other cases converts are attacked, beaten or thrown out of their homes or jobs. Sometimes their spouses and children are taken away.

Converting to Christianity can be an extremely dangerous and traumatic experience for Muslims. Many converts may have to go into hiding for fear of their lives. Christians must realise that they have a duty to look after converts as many of them will no longer have homes, families or jobs. The local church must become the convert's new family and this may mean providing safe places to hide, accommodation, food, friendship, fellowship and even financial help or a job. Most importantly converts must be welcomed into the church as fellow believers. They should never be considered or treated as outcasts or second-class Christians.

Christians must also understand that public declarations of faith or open-air baptisms may be very dangerous for converts. They may be seen by Muslim communities who may try to punish converts by beating them or even killing them. Sometimes Muslim communities react to public demonstrations of faith by converts by starting riots and attacking Christian buildings and churches.

Discipleship

It says in Matthew 28: 19-20 that the Lord Jesus has commanded us to make disciples of all nations and teach them what He has taught us. Once a Muslim has been brought to Christ they should not be left to fend for themselves. It is so important that a convert is cared for and taught what it means to be a follower of Christ. As we have seen in this course, Islam is very different from Christianity. For most converts Islam is all they have known so the discipleship process may be slow as they learn more about Christ and

Christianity and living as a Christian. It is important that they become part of a Bible study or home group that will be sensitive to their need to learn about the basics of Christianity. Many people say that it takes some converts as long as two years to be discipled properly. Pastors, church leaders and friends should continue to pray with and for them and act as helpers.

Some questions to think about or discuss

- Despite our differences how must we treat Muslims?

  ....

  ....

- What does Matthew 28: 18-20 teach us about witnessing to others?

  ....

  ....

- What things should we pray for before and after meeting Muslim friends?

  ....

  ....

- What important things should you remember when making friends with Muslims?

  ....

  ....

- What should women especially remember about Muslim men?

  ....

  ....

- What things should you share about your faith to your Muslim friends?

  ....

  ....

- What useful questions could you ask your Muslim friend for them to consider accepting Christ into their lives?

  ....

  ....

- Why is it dangerous for Muslims to convert to Christianity?

  ....

  ....

- As Christians how should we care for converts?

  ....

  ....

- What does Matthew 28: 19-20 teach us about converts?

  ....

  ....

- What will you do now to make friends with Muslims in your own life?

  ....

  ....

Glossary

adhan	the call to prayer
Ahl al-Kitab	People of the Book (i.e. Jews and Christians)
Allah	the Arabic word for "God", also used by Arab Christians
amir	commander, leader or prince
arkan al-din	the five pillars of Islam
asr	the afternoon prayer (third prayer time of the day)
ayah	a verse in the Quran
Ayatollah	a term of honour for a Shia religious leader
Berbers	the indigenous peoples of North Africa. Many were Christians in the pre-Islamic period but were Islamised by the Arab Muslim conquerors in the 7th century and joined with them in the Muslim expansion into Europe
bismillah	in the name of Allah
burqa	garment some Muslim women wear in public which covers their whole body and face
Byzantine	the Byzantine Empire (324-1453) was the Eastern part of the Roman Empire, which lasted nearly 1,000 years after the Western Roman Empire had come to an end. Its capital was Constantinople, its language was Greek and its religion Christianity. It saw itself as the defender of Christianity against the paganism and Islam
caliph	Sunni word for the supreme political and religious leader of the Muslim community. Shia Muslims use the word "imam"
Dajjal	Antichrist
Dar al-Harb	House of War, that is, territory not under Islamic rule
Dar al-Islam	House of Islam; territory that is under Islamic rule
dawa	Islamic mission
dhimmi	In Islamic law, this term is used for Christians and Jews who live in Muslim countries. They are treated as second class citizens
din	religious rituals
dua	voluntary prayers
fajr	the dawn prayer (first prayer of the day)
fard	obligatory
fatiha	the first sura of the Quran
fatwa	a published decision taken by Muslim religious leaders about Islamic law or doctrine
ghusl	the ritual washing of some parts of the body required before prayer
hadith	a collection of traditions or stories about Muhammad's life, treated as holy scripture by Muslims and second only to the Quran

hajj	the annual pilgrimage to Mecca that Muslims have to complete once in their life times if they can afford it. One of the five pillars of Islam
hajji	a Muslim who has gone on pilgrimage to Mecca
hijab	a cloth Muslim women use to cover their hair and neck
hijra	Muhammad's flight from Mecca to Medina in 622 AD. This date is used as the starting point for the Islamic calendar
Iblis	one of the names of the devil
Id al-Fitr	the feast at the end of the month long fast of Ramadan
iftar	the meal at the end of each day's fast during Ramadan
imam	leader of a mosque (In Shia Islam imam means the leader of all Shia Muslims worldwide)
iman	faith believed and declared
Injil	what Muslims call the Christian Gospels or sometimes the whole New Testament
iqra	read or recite
Isa	Islamic name for Jesus
isha	the night prayer (the fifth prayer of the day)
Islamists	radical Muslims; those who want to set up Islamic states under sharia law in every country of the world (see pages 40-41)
Janissaries	the best troops of the Ottoman Empire, they were Christian boys taken forcefully from their families, converted to Islam and trained to fight
janna	literally "the garden"; a term used for paradise or heaven
jihad	literally "striving". The term has a number of meanings in Islam including: (1) spiritual struggle for moral purity; (2) trying to correct wrong and support right by words and actions; (3) holy war against non-Muslims with the aim of spreading Islam across the world
jinn	a spirit created by Allah. There are some good jinn but many are evil
jizya	tax paid by dhimmi as a sign of submission to Muslims
jumma	Friday, the Muslim holy day
Kaaba	cube-shaped holy shrine in Mecca
kabira	great sins
khutba	address (sermon) at Friday mid-day prayers
kismat	fate, destiny
maghrib	sunset, the evening prayer (fourth prayer time of the day)
Mahdi	literally "rightly guided one". Muslims are waiting for his return at the End Time
maktub	"it is written" (expression of fatalism)
malaikah	angels
maqdur	"it is decided" (expression of fatalism)

marabout	a religious leader who is involved in occultic powers. The term is used mostly in North and West Africa
mizan	scales on which good and bad deeds are weighed
Mongol	the Mongols were nomadic tribes from the region of modern-day Mongolia. In 1206 they united under one leader, Genghis Khan. Soon they began to send armies out in every direction to conquer other lands and create a huge empire. Gradually many Mongols converted to Islam
muezzin	the one who gives out the call to prayer from the mosque
mufti	highly respected Sunni scholar who can interpret laws and issue fatwas
mujahidin	those who go on jihad; Islamic warriors
mullah	religious teacher
muta	a short term marriage contract in Shia Islam
nabi	prophet
nikah	marriage
niqab	cloth covering face, hair and neck of a Muslim woman
Ottoman	The Muslim Ottoman Empire (1299–1923) was founded by Osman I who ruled a small Muslim Turkic sultanate in Anatolia (modern-day Turkey). The Ottomans tried constantly to expand into the Christian Byzantine Empire and Europe. At the height of its power (in the 16th and 17th centuries) the Ottoman Empire controlled much of south-eastern Europe, the Middle East and North Africa
pir	Sufi spiritual guide
qibla	the direction of prayer i.e. towards Mecca
Quran	Islamic holy book
Ramadan	the ninth month of the Muslim calendar, the fasting month
rasul	messenger of God; apostle
saghira	little sins
salah	compulsory Muslim ritual prayer recited five times a day
salam	literally "peace"; used as a greeting
sawm	the act of fasting
Seljuks	a Turkic tribe from Central Asia who converted to Islam and migrated into Muslim regions in the 11th century and set up the Empire of the Great Seljuks. They won a great victory over the Byzantines in 1071 and then moved into Anatolia (the area of modern Turkey) in large numbers where they established the Seljuk Sultanate of Rum
shahada	Islamic declaration of faith
sharia	Islamic law
Shaytan	Satan, one of the names of the devil
sheikh	Islamic elder or scholar; also used to mean a Sufi spiritual guide
Shia	the Muslim sect that believes that the rightful successors to Muhammad were the descendants of Ali

shirk	associating anyone with Allah as co-god; it is the worst sin in Islam
Sufi	a Muslim mystic
sunna	the life, customs and examples of Muhammad which Muslims should follow without question
Sunni	Muslims who accept the first four caliphs as rightly guided and legitimate. They believe a caliph must always be from Muhammad's tribe
sura	a chapter in the Quran
talaq	divorce
taqiyya	a doctrine that allows Muslims to deny their faith in order to escape persecution. It has been extended to permit lying or deception in order to spread Islam
tasbih	a Muslim rosary
Tatar	the Tatars were Mongol and Turkic tribes who established a state known as the Khanate of the Golden Horde based on the Volga basin. It converted to Islam towards the end of the 13th century and expanded into the Russian steppes and Eastern Europe
Taurah	the Torah, the law of Moses, the first five books of the Old Testament
tawhid	the Islamic belief that God one and cannot be divided. This belief opposes Christian teaching on the Trinity and Christian teaching that Jesus is God
tayammum	purification by sand or earth (when water is not available for washing)
ulama	Islamic scholars
umma	the whole body of Muslims worldwide
Wahhabis	followers of a very strict form of Islam
Yawm al-Akhirah	the Day of Judgement
Zabur	Psalms
zakat	giving to support Islam
zuhr	the mid-day prayer (second prayer time of the day)

Barnabas Fund

who we are

barnabasfund
hope and aid for the persecuted church

As part of the family of God, Barnabas Fund stands with our Christian brothers and sisters around the world, where they are in the minority and suffer discrimination, oppression and persecution as a result of their faith.

- We encourage prayer by Christians for their suffering brothers and sisters.

- We provide practical aid to transform the lives of persecuted Christians, encouraging donations from individuals and churches and channelling funds through local ministries and Christian organisations.

- We tell the untold story about the plight of persecuted Christians around the world. We also raise awareness about the challenge that Islam poses to the Church, its mission, and society.

- We speak out on behalf of Christians suffering injustice and violence, addressing religious and secular ideologies that deny full religious liberty to Christian minorities – while continuing to show God's love to all people.

- We witness to the love of Christ and seek to build His Kingdom.

International Headquarters
The Old Rectory, River Street,
Pewsey, Wiltshire SN9 5DB, UK
Telephone 01672 564938
Fax 01672 565030
From outside the UK
Telephone +44 1672 564938
Fax +44 1672 565030
Email info@barnabasfund.org

UK
9 Priory Row,
Coventry CV1 5EX
Telephone 024 7623 1923
Fax 024 7683 4718
From outside the UK
Telephone +44 24 7623 1923
Fax +44 24 7683 4718
Email info@barnabasfund.org

Australia
Postal Suite 107, 236 Hyperdome,
Loganholme QLD 4129
Telephone (07) 3806 1076
or 1300 365 799
Fax (07) 3806 4076
Email bfaustralia@barnabasfund.org

Jersey
Le Jardin, La Rue A Don, Grouville,
Jersey, Channel Islands JE3 9GB
Telephone 700600
Fax 700601
Email bfjersey@barnabasfund.org

New Zealand
PO Box 27 6018,
Manukau City,
Auckland, 2241
Telephone (09) 280 4385
Email office@barnabasfund.org.nz

USA
6731 Curran St,
McLean, VA 22101
Telephone (703) 288-1681 or
toll-free 1-866-936-2525
Fax (703) 288-1682
Email usa@barnabasaid.org

www.barnabasfund.org   (in USA) www.barnabasaid.org